DATA MINING

Your Ultimate Guide to a Comprehensive Understanding of Data Mining

Liam Damien

Table of Contents

Introduction 1

Chapter 1: What is Data Mining?..................................8

    Importance of Data Mining 10

Chapter 2: Applications of Data Mining? 12

    Retail and Service 12

    Manufacturing.. 14

    Finance and Insurance.. 14

    Transport 14

    Healthcare and Medical Industry 15

    Property 15

    Telecommunication and Utilities 15

Chapter 3: Steps on How to Do Data Mining? 17

    Step 1: Define the Problem 17

    Step 2: Data Integration 18

    Step 3: Data Selection... 18

    Step 4: Data Cleaning 19

    Step 5: Data Transformation 22

    Step 6: Data Mining 24

Step 7: Pattern Evaluation 25

Step 8: Knowledge Presentation 25

Chapter 4: Data Mining Techniques **26**

Descriptive Mining Techniques 26

Predictive Mining Techniques 29

Chapter 5: Association Rule Discovery **36**

How Association Rule Discovery Works 37

Association Rule Algorithms 38

Use of Association Rules in Data Mining 39

Chapter 6: Decision Trees **44**

What of The Decision Tree Algorithm Pseudocodes? 46

Attributes Selection 48

Information Gain 49

Steps Involved in Building a Decision Tree 50

Chapter 7: Data Integration **52**

Understanding Data Integration in the Real World 53

Issues Associated with the Process
of Data Integration and Their Solutions 54

Chapter 8: Data Transformation **59**

Stage 1 59

Stage 2 60

Why Transform Data? 60

How is Data Transformed? 62

What are Some of the Data Transformation Challenges? 63

Data Transformation Techniques 64

Data transformation best practices... 67

Chapter 9: Data Warehousing 74

Data Warehouse Types.. 75

Using Data Warehouse Information... 76

How to Integrate Heterogeneous Databases........................... 77

Data Warehouse Tools and Utility Functions........................... 79

Why is a Data Warehouse Separated from Operational
Databases? 82

Features of a Data Warehouse.. 83

Applications of the Data Warehouse 84

Key takeaways 85

Chapter 10: Data Mining Challenges..86

Noisy Data... 89

Distributed/Scattered Data 90

Complex Data Restructuring 90

Algorithm Performance 91

Incorporating Background Knowledge 91

Data Protection, Data Privacy 91

Data Mining Trends 92

Chapter 11: Data Mining Tools 94

Rapid Miner 94

Orange 95

Weka 97

KNIME 97

Sisense 98

SQL Server data tools (SSDT) 99

Apache Mahout 100

Oracle Data Mining.. 101

Rattle 101

DataMelt... 102

IBM Cognos... 103

IBM SPSS Modeler 103

SAS Data Mining 104

Teradata... 105

Board 105

Dundas BI.. 106

Chapter 12: Text Mining in Data Mining: Process and Applications 107

Information Extraction 108

Data Mining 108

Natural Language Processing (NLP)................................. 109

Information Extraction 109

Text mining process.. 110

Approaches to Text Mining in Data Mining..................... 111

How Do You Numericize Texts?....................................... 114

Incorporating Text Mining Results 116

Advantages of Text Mining... 118

Disadvantages of Text Mining 119

Chapter 13: Data Modeling in Data Mining? 121

Why Use Data Models? 122

Types of Data models 123

Data Modeling Approaches 127

Advantages of Data Models 130

Disadvantages of Data Models 131

Chapter 14: Data Mining and the Current Market 132

Data Mining Market Size 132

SAS 133

SPSS 133

IBM 134

Microsoft Corporation 134

Oracle 135

Angoss 135

KXEN 136

Chapter 15: New Trends in Data Mining? 137

Embedded Data Mining 138

Data Mining Packages for Vertical Applications 138

Product Consolidation 139

PMML 140

Multimedia Data Mining 140

Ubiquitous Data Mining 141

Distributed Data Mining 141

Spatial and Geographical Data Mining 141

Trends in Data Mining Techniques 142

Seeking Out Incomplete Data 142

Dynamic Data Dashboards 143

Database Analysis 143

Text Analysis 143

Efficient Handling of Complex and Relational Data 143

Relevance and Scalability of Selected Data Mining Algorithms144

Conclusion **145**

Introduction

Have you been sifting through piles of data trying to find useful information? If you are looking for ways to do data mining, you are in the right place.

One thing that is important to note is that data mining employs artificial intelligence (AI) techniques, advanced statistical tools, and neural networks. With the use of these sophisticated data mining techniques, one can learn about patterns, trends, and relationships that might have been unknown before. What you need to bear in mind is that data mining aims at unraveling hidden rules that underlie the data.

Think of data mining as data surfing or data digging.

You dig through something because you are looking for something hidden inside, right? Well, data mining is more like data digging. What you are trying to do is to discover connections that you did not know existed. Then you can use these connections to make predictions about future trends.

Data mining is a phenomenon that was not coined until the 1990s, when it was still referred to as knowledge discovery in databases. There are three major scientific disciplines that form the basis of data mining. These disciplines are intertwined with one another. These disciplines include artificial intelligence, statistics, and machine learning.

But what are these disciplines, anyway?

Well, statistics refer to the numeric study that unravels relationships between data. Artificial intelligence, on the other hand, is the human-like intelligence that is displayed by machines and software. Machine learning refers to the use of algorithms that can learn from the data and then use that to make predictions.

Today, what was once old is new again! This is because data mining technologies are rapidly evolving to keep up with the unlimited potential big data has to offer as well as affordable computing power.

In other words, computers have advanced processing power and speed, which has played a central role in allowing us to move beyond manual, time-consuming, and labor-intensive practices. This way, data analysis is done fast, easy, and automatically.

As more and more complex datasets are being collected, the more the potential to unravel relevant insights. Look around you at banks, retailers, telecommunication providers, manufacturers, and insurers, among others, how do they handle their data?

The truth is that they use data mining to unravel important relationships among them so that it can inform price optimization, demographics, and promotions. All these factors are essential in decision making as to how the economy, social media, competition, and risk affect their business models, customer relationships, revenue generation, and operations.

So, if you are an aspiring entrepreneur, data mining should not scare you. Rather than looking at it as something complex and too technical, think of it as a bridge from where you are to the other side of success (where you want to be).

Data makes the whole difference. You cannot eliminate the implementation of applications, intelligence methodologies, and technologies. You need data mining to gather, analyze, and interpret data for relevant information about the market, business operations, and the industry as a whole. In other words, data mining is an essential component of business intelligence.

Data Mining and Business Intelligence

2019 has been marked with the exponential growth in the digital universe. It is these turns of events that promise some exciting technological advancements and improvements in the data mining field.

When you think business, there are two phenomena you cannot escape - data mining and business intelligence. These two factors play a central role in determining the growth and success of any valuable business. Despite the fact that these terms are often used interchangeably, one thing you need to bear in mind is that business intelligence and data mining are distinct from each other within the data technologies spectrum.

Just as an introduction, business intelligence is what offers a deeper insight into both your business and that of your rivals/competitors. It is concerned with the collection and processing of large volumes of data, whether through internal metrics or third-party resources.

On the other hand, data mining is concerned with the analysis of data for the purpose of identifying useful patterns and insights. It is through the use of various software that companies are able to analyze information from a wide range of sources with the aim of identifying trends. Just to translate this into layman terms, business intelligence works by transforming raw data into useful information that you can action in any business. Data mining on the other hand, just as the name suggests, is the mining of useful information. The major difference between these two phenomena is the form of style each employs.

In other words, while business intelligence uses metrics tracking in deriving useful information, data mining on the other hand uses computational intelligence and algorithms in the identification of useful patterns. One thing you need to understand is that business intelligence plays a central role in aiding decision-making while data mining answers more specific questions concerning a business.

It is because of this that data mining capabilities are today utilized in fueling business intelligence efforts. Note that big data in itself is transformed into business intelligence when used in spotting opportunities about the future of any company. There are so many steps that you have to follow to turn raw data into useful intelligence.

The most important thing you need to note is that to maximize profits from data mining, business leaders need to understand why and how information is gathered. They also have to understand how to use the information acquired in making managerial and operational decisions.

Taking data mining and business intelligence as the backbone of any successful business is the way to go. So, if you have not yet done that, it is time to hop onto the bandwagon. These are the major trends you are looking at:

Artificial Intelligence

Looking back to 2018, artificial intelligence dominated the industry with research revealing that at least 38% of businesses already implemented AI in one way or another. Companies that had not adopted AI were already falling behind and had to catch up with their competitors already using the technology. One thing you need to note is that industries already using AI are able to collect and process data, making it easier for effective data mining and the making of informed business decisions.

It is important to note that AI platforms contribute to the evaluation of data inputs much quicker than humans do. They are also able to detect errors that would have otherwise been hard to note when using the human eye. While so many skeptics today label AI in data mining and business intelligence as a temporary fad, statistics demonstrate otherwise. And that is exactly what we have witnessed in 2019 and are likely to see it go on in 2020 and beyond.

Self-Service Business Intelligence

You may be wondering what self-service business intelligence is all about. Well, think of it as something that permits companies to dive directly into analytics without necessarily bringing in an external data scientist. In 2019, we have already witnessed self-service intelligence produce more analysis information than data scientists. This explains the reason why it has been adopted largely by small businesses that often do not shave their budgets to hire external help.

Let's consider the example of Insights by Google My Business. What is interesting is that the insight panel found within your GMB dashboard offers business owners with data on customer engagement. This data is derived from the GMB listing, offering data on the number of views each listing has and the number of clients who interact with the listing, the location data as well as phone call volumes associated with that.

Data Retention

While so many companies would prefer to store their data for backup for a specific duration, the chances are that they will not hold on to it forever. In this case, machine learning is taught to clean the stored data and dispose of anything that is no longer required. Think of it as an automated data flash, thanks to data mining software and techniques.

Data Governance

In the 2019 poll, there were more than 2,600 respondents that demonstrated data governance. Well, based on the industry you work in, emphasis on data governance differs with telecommunications and banking. Data governance goes a long way in providing businesses with valuable insight through its data as well as business intelligence efforts.

In other words, if the data is inaccurate or duplicated, this would be considered poor quality, which would contribute to a lack of credibility and confidence in company leadership. This would, in turn, make the focus on BI (Business Intelligence) unworthwhile. As such, data governance is critical in healthcare where, if data is compromised or inaccurate, it can contribute to severe legal and medical repercussions.

As there is more data being moved to remote servers and AI is catching on steadily in the data mining field, the healthcare industry, among others, is starting to understand the fact that medical data is soon going to move into Big Data space. However, the shift is being slowed by HIPAA and privacy concerns.

Chapter 1

What is Data Mining?

This is one of the questions you will hear people asking on social media, news headlines, educational forums, and other platforms. Data mining is defined as the exploration and analysis of data with the main aim of discovering meaningful rules, patterns, and future trends.

It is thought of as a discipline under the field of data science. It is quite different from predictive analytics since that aims to give a description of historical data, while data mining concerns itself with predicting possible outcomes in the future. It is through data mining techniques that machine learning (ML) models are built so that they can power modern AI applications. These applications include search engine algorithms as well as recommendation systems.

So many businesses consider data mining as a proven technology and a critical factor in business decision making. Many cases and case studies offer the capacity to mine and analyze data. Shockingly, there are so many implementation failures reported in this field, which has led to businesses misplacing their business priorities and clouding business objectives.

While reported implementations are battling through these challenges, some have failed in delivering the right data insights and their usefulness to the business. In this book, we are going to throw some light on how you can successfully implement data mining projects.

As we have already mentioned, data mining helps in uncovering hidden patterns in large structured datasets and then using them to predict future outcomes. Think of structured data as data that is organized into rows and columns. This allows such data to be accessed with ease and their modification to be done efficiently.

If you are smart, you can use machine learning algorithms to mine data for a variety of use cases. This will help you avoid risks, reduce costs, and improve revenues. What you need to bear in mind is that, at its core, data mining is composed of two principal functions - description and prediction. The description is all about interpreting large databases, while prediction is concerned with finding insights, like relationships and patterns in known values.

How do you decide on the data mining approach to use? Well, the answer lies in what your business objective is and what value creation you intend to drive. When you have a complete blend of business understanding and technical capabilities, you are certainly going to make big data projects, both successful and valuable.

There are five significant elements of data mining. These include extraction, data storage & management, data access for analysts, data analysis using a wide range of tools, technologies and software, and data presentation in a more understandable format for the general audience.

Importance of Data Mining

As far as data is concerned, organizations, businesses, and industries share similar challenges. If you ask any organization, the probable response would be that they cannot find the data they need. However, even if they knew where to find it, they might not know how to get their hands on it.

On the other hand, some have access to the data but cannot seem to understand what it means. The worst thing is, the data they need may be readily available to them and they can understand it. However, for some reason, they cannot put that data into good use.

Well, if your company falls into one of the categories mentioned, then understand that there is hope for you. In other words, this is where data mining comes in to play.

One of the main reasons why data mining is essential is the fact that it facilitates the conversion of data from its raw form to processed form/information. It is this processed form of data that is then converted into knowledge one can use when making critical business decisions.

Recently, many companies across the world have faced the problem of data explosion. In other words, there is a sudden surge in data production, causing an increase in demand and a subsequent increase in the amount of information and knowledge. This means that there is a need for this kind of expansion to be quickly, effectively, and efficiently processed into a form that can be consumed. The good news is that data mining offers that solution. You can think of data mining as a long-awaited solution.

It is expected that organizations and business enterprises that maintain such massive databases employ the use of data mining. The truth is, such a sheer size of the database and its corresponding amount of information requires an equal measure of organization and analysis that can only come from data mining.

It is through data mining that users and analysts can look at the data from varied points of view when conducting their analysis. This will also make it easier to put processed information into categories based on such features as patterns, correlations, and relationships, among others.

Chapter 2

Applications of Data Mining?

The use of data mining techniques is something that can be witnessed in so many business sectors and industries:

Retail and Service

In the service and retail sectors, the sale of consumer goods and services gives rise to large amounts of data. The primary role of data mining techniques in this sector is to improve the ability of the company to drive proper customer relationships, supply chain, financial, procurement, and core operations management. The most common areas where data mining is useful in the industry includes:

Product Pricing

Data mining plays a critical role in product pricing policies, as well as price models.

Promotion Effectiveness Analysis

This is where the company is responsible for gathering and analyzing data from previous campaigns and promotions along with the benefits and costs the campaigns offered the company. What this does is provides insight into the key elements responsible for increasing the success of future promotions and campaigns.

Profitability Analysis

Here, data mining goes a long way in evaluating and comparing various branches, stores, and other business units of the company. This way, the management is in a better position of identifying what areas are profitable in the business so that they can make appropriate decisions.

Customer Segmentation Analysis

Data mining techniques will help companies look at customer feedback and classify them into segments to identify a sudden shift in demographics, among other segmentation outcomes.

Budgetary Analysis

This is where companies are interested in getting a clear comparison of their expenditures, relative to their budgeted expenses. The good news is that the knowledge derived from data mining will go a long way in informing budgeting for subsequent quarters.

Inventory Control

Here, data mining plays a significant role in monitoring and analyzing the level of inventory movements relative to lot sizes and safety stocks. Additionally, data mining also gives more insight into the lead-time analysis.

Manufacturing

Just like in the areas of retail and service industry, data mining is also applied in similar areas of the manufacturing industry. However, one thing you will note about the manufacturing industry is that it uses data mining to inform quality improvement (QI) initiatives.

In other words, data obtained from quality improvement programs, like Kaizen and Six Sigma, are analyzed. The results are then used in resolving product quality issues that the company faces.

Finance and Insurance

If you look at banks, among other financial organizations, data mining is actively used as a critical component of business intelligence initiatives. However, data mining is mostly used in risk management. In other words, it is used to determine and subsequently lower the credit and market risks financial institutions are often faced with. Other risks include operational and liquidity risks, which are uncovered using data mining tools.

On the other hand, data mining is often used to conduct credit analysis of customers. Insurance companies also use these kinds of tools when conducting claims and fraud analysis.

Transport

It is important to note that the transport industry is often concerned about logistics, making it one of the areas where data mining is extensively applied. Because of this, logistics management benefits hugely from the use of data mining techniques. Various states and governments are also using data mining tools for such activities as traffic control, road construction, and rehabilitation, among others.

Healthcare and Medical Industry

Each day, experiments, studies, and research reveal that there are tons of data generated in the healthcare and medical industry. It is through the use of data mining that these experiments, researches, and studies see the light of day.

Property

One important point to note is that the real estate industry cannot be thriving without relevant information gleaned from property evaluation, thanks to data mining. Here, the bottom line is not entirely on sales; instead, it is on property valuation trends over the years as well as the appraisal comparisons.

Telecommunication and Utilities

Various organizations that deal with utility services are recipients of data mining benefits. For instance, most telecommunication companies do record analysis. The electric and water companies are interested in electricity and water usage, and data mining plays a huge role in conducting consumption analysis.

Additionally, with the growing popularity of cellular phones, all transactions and information have become a playground for security threats from hackers. This is what spurred the invention of coral systems that are meant to bust fraudsters. It is through data mining that these fraudsters can be tracked down through their cellular usage patterns analysis when doing fraudulent activities.

Chapter 3

Steps on How to Do Data Mining?

There are a series of steps that you need to go through when doing data mining. Some people pack this process into five steps. However, I have chosen to break the process into eight steps for you to appreciate and understand what each entails.

Step 1: Define the Problem

The first thing you need to do, before getting started with anything, is to determine what your objectives are as far as the data mining process is concerned. Ask yourself what it is that you aim to accomplish with the data mining process. Ask yourself what problem you have and would like to address? Is there something your business or organization will benefit from the whole data mining process? Having a perspective on what the problem, objectives, and justification is for doing data mining plays a role in informing what techniques and tools to employ.

Step 2: Data Integration

Data integration begins with raw data for the activity, transaction, item, or event. The main goal here is to offer the users a unified perspective of the data irrespective of whether they are derived from single or multiple sources.

Here, you will need to:

Identify All Possible Sources of Data

One thing you will note is that the initial list of references will possibly be heterogeneous and long. The most important thing is that you integrate all these sources to save on time and resources needed later in the process.

Collect the Data

Now that you have identified all the sources, the next thing is for you to gather data from all the sources you identified and integrated. Those that you derive from multiple sources can be merged.

That said, data integration plays a central role in lowering the potential number and frequency of duplication and redundancy found in datasets. This way, you have a chance to improve both the accuracy and speed of data mining.

Step 3: Data Selection

Once you are done with the first two steps, the chances are that you might be faced with a considerable chunk irrelevant data. In other words, you have a massive chunk of your data that will not help address the problem you seek to solve.

This means that you cannot use that data, hence the need to weed it out. This way, you remain with the data that is relevant and useful in answering your research questions or meeting your set objectives.

Therefore, you will need to:

Create a Target Dataset

The target dataset you create will play a significant role in establishing critical parameters of your data that are necessary for data mining.

Select the Data

Once you have gathered your data, the next thing is for you to identify what set falls within the category you are targeting. This is the subset you will be subjected to pre-processing.

Step 4: Data Cleaning

In most cases, you will hear people referring to data cleaning as data cleansing or data scrubbing. Here, data that you have selected for pre-processing will be cleaned before it can be subjected to other data mining techniques. Some books consider the data cleaning step as the first step in the two-step pre-processing phase.

You have to bear in mind that errors, inconsistencies, and inaccuracies characterize any data that is obtained in its raw form.

Some are incomplete or have missing values. In short, the quality of such a dataset is considered compromised. Because of these reasons, there is a need for such a dataset to be cleaned up. Remember that if your data is of poor quality, then the results you will obtain are unrealizable and hence, unfit for data mining.

One thing that might be racing through your mind is what possible reason could it be for all these kinds of errors.

Well, one of the most significant contributors to these errors is the source of the data. In other words, if the data came from a single source, some of the typical quality issues that will need cleaning include:

Data Entry Errors

This is usually attributed to human error. When someone is inputting data into the data warehouse, they may key in incorrect data when typing. These errors can range from spelling mistakes, duplication of entries to data redundancies.

Naming Conflict

This is often a problem that results from having multiple sources of the same data but are named differently. The risk here is that of data duplication comes from one sample being named differently. Alternative, there are cases where more than one data source uses the same name for two different sets of data, which are entirely unrelated.

Lack of Integrity Constraints

This includes such features as referential integrity and uniqueness. Considering that there is only one source, there is no way to ascertain whether the data is unique or not. Because of this, data is duplicated or inconsistent. In the same way, data that is obtained from varied sources may end up with quality problems.

Inconsistent Timing

This happens where data overlaps with each other bringing a lot of confusion. This renders the data unreliable. For instance, when you look at data derived from a client's shopping history, it may overlap with that obtained from other sites they have shopped in.

Inconsistent Aggregation

This is a contradiction that happens from obtaining data from varied sources. Duplication of data often results in them canceling each other out.

That said, data cleaning often involves such activities as data profiling. The main aim of profiling your data is to determine the statistics and information about them to ascertain the actual content, structure, and quality.

Other techniques you can employ include clustering. Once the data is cleaned, there will be no need to update the record because what you have is a clean version you can work with.

Step 5: Data Transformation

This is considered as the second step of data pre-processing. Other authors consider this to be a part of the data cleaning process.

That said, once you have cleaned your dataset, the truth is that it might still be unavailable for mining. This means that you have to transform it so that it is ready for extraction. To do this, you have to convert the source data format of your data into "destination data." This is the format that is usable and recognizable to the data mining tools/techniques.

Some of the standard transformation techniques you can employ include:

Smoothing

This is a fundamental technique used in eliminating the noise and inconsistencies in data. But what is noise? Well, this refers to random errors and variance in your measured variables. The process of smoothing involves the performance of tasks and operations involved in data cleaning. These are:

Binning

Smoothing is achieved by using the neighborhood of data values chosen. This is then distributed categorically in the bins. Here, neighborhoods refer to values that lie around the selected data values. Therefore, by sorting the values in the bins, you will be able to smooth out all the noise.

Clustering

This is an operation that is conducted by merely organizing values into groups/clusters based on specific features or variables. In other words, the similar data values will be placed under one cluster. This way, the data noise is smoothed out or eliminated.

Regression

This is another method you can use to smooth out noise from your data. Linear regression often goes a long way in determining the best line of fit for two variables. In the process, the predictive value is improved. On the other hand, multiple regression works by finding the best line of fit in more than two variables.

Aggregation

This is one of the techniques that play a significant role in reducing the bulk and streamlining the data mining process by applying summarization tactics. It is often used when creating data cubes that are used in downstream data analysis. An excellent example of this is how retail companies make their summaries of their sales data periodically in every duration of time. This helps in creating daily, weekly, monthly, and annual sales data.

Normalization

This is also referred to as standardization. It is important to note that variations in data can have an impact on its quality. For instance, if you have gaps in your data, this can cause problems when mining.

This means that each dataset has to be normalized first by simply specifying an acceptance range, otherwise referred to as a standard. The data is then scaled up to ensure that they fall within the acceptable range using Min-Max normalization limits, normalizing by decimal scaling, and Z-score normalization methods among others.

Generalization

This is much like aggregation because it causes a reduction in data size. Here, raw data is identified and then replaced with a higher-level data. For instance, data values on the client age can be replaced by higher data groupings such as pre-teens, teens, juniors, and seniors, among others.

Similarly, the raw data on annual family income can be generalized and transformed into higher-level concepts such as low-income, middle-class income, high-income, and wealthy level families, among others.

Step 6: Data Mining

Now that your data is clean and transformed into a destination format that can be mined, the next thing is for data mining to happen. The aim here is to determine the pattern, relationship, and correlation within and among the datasets in the database.

This is considered the core of the whole data mining process. It often entails the extraction of data patterns by employing varied methods and operations. The choice of what data approach to use is mostly dependent on what the objective is for performing data mining. We will discuss some of the standard data mining techniques in the next chapter.

Step 7: Pattern Evaluation

The next thing is to curate the patterns, relationships and correlations derived in the previous step. Here, you will need to inspect, analyze, and evaluate these patterns.

The process of evaluation is by evaluating how interesting the parameters/measures are. This enables you to determine what patterns are truly interesting, impactful or relevant to give useful information. Once you interpret the outcome of this step, this marks the transformation of data into a large bag of knowledge you can use in making informed business decisions.

Step 8: Knowledge Presentation

Here, the knowledge you derive from the evaluation and interpretation of data mining patterns has to be presented to the relevant stakeholders. The best way to do this presentation is through the use of visualization techniques, among other knowledge representation mechanisms. Once that is done, this knowledge may be used in policymaking and business decisions-making.

Chapter 4

Data Mining Techniques

As the concept of data mining evolves, there is a significant advancement in technology as more and more tools and techniques are introduced to improve data analysis. As mentioned in the 5th step of data mining, there is a need for various methods for mining transformed data.

Some of the techniques that you can use include the following:

Descriptive Mining Techniques

Clustering/Cluster Analysis

This is one of the oldest data mining techniques. It is also considered the most straightforward and effective technique to use in data mining. Here, what you need to do is classify data of values that possess common characteristics or have similarities of some sort. These groupings create subsets that are otherwise referred to as clusters.

This kind of clustering is natural. In other words, there are no pre-defined groups of classes of data values that are distributed.

An excellent example of where this is used is in market research, specifically in market segmentation. This is where the market is clustered into unique segments. For instance, you can have a cosmetic manufacturing company producing female skincare products grouping its clients into sections based on such factors as age. In such a case, the most likely clusters you will have may include teens, young adults, middle age, senior and mature adults, among others.

Association Rule Discovery

The main aim is to give a more in-depth insight into how data values in an extensive database are related or correlated with each other. This in turn reveals the association or how data is bound to one another. The data analysis, in this case, is achieved by examining the patterns and correlations that exist.

One of the common examples where association rule is applied in data mining is that of customer behavior. Here, businesses evaluate the behavior of their clients so that they can inform decision making in product price points and features offered.

Apart from this technique being descriptive, it is also predictive. This is especially the case when you use it in predicting the behavior of customers in response to specific changes. For instance, when a company decides to launch a new product on the market, you would want to know how the product will be received. The association rule will play a significant role in hypothesizing how customers are likely to accept the newly introduced product in the market.

Sequential Pattern Discovery

This technique is slightly similar to the association rule. This is because they both aim at unraveling interesting associations or relationships in data values present in the database. However, unlike the former method, this technique puts into consideration the sequence within the transaction and even the company.

Additionally, this method is often applied to data that are contained in sequence databases. In the example we gave above on client behavior, this may help a great deal in painting a detailed picture of the events that clients follow when buying. There may be a precise sequence on what product they buy first, second, third, all the way to the nth product.

Concept/Class Description

This is often a straightforward technique that pays attention to the characterization and discrimination of data. This explains the reason why it is also called Characterization and discrimination technique. Here, the features of data are simply generalized, summarized, and then compared and contrasted.

It is expected that a data mining system generates a descriptive summary of features or data values, otherwise referred to as data characterization.

For instance, if a company is planning its operations overseas and has no idea what location best suits the business, this would be the method to use. This will help determine what sites overseas they should have their branches (i.e., what county). Should they go for one that is dry and arid all year round? Should they go for a wet stormy one half of the year?

The data drawn from the two regions will be examined for their descriptions, then compared to determine what their similarities and differences are.

Predictive Mining Techniques

Classification

This is quite similar to the clustering technique we discussed in the sections above. Most people often think of them as the same thing. However, there is a slight difference between them because here, classes, groups, or instances are already pre-determined.

In the case of clustering, the groups are often defined first before data values are put into their respective clusters. In classification, the data values are sorted into the already pre-determined clusters.

Additionally, data values are segregated into groups, which are then used in making predictions on how each one of the data values is likely to behave. The behavior is based on how other values within that class behave.

A good example is used in medical research when analyzing common diseases for specific countries. In such a case, the classification of diseases is already known. What is left unknown is data collection based on symptoms of the population and then subsequently classifying them into disease clusters where they fit.

Nearest Neighbor Joining Analysis

This technique is quite similar to the clustering technique we discussed earlier. This is mainly because it involves taking a selected set of data values based on other values around it. While clustering often involves data values that are in proximity to each other, hence belonging to the same cluster. In other words, the nearest neighbors are more on the nearness of data values being compared to the selected dataset.

Let us consider an example of the cosmetic and skincare products manufacturing company we discussed earlier. In such a case, Nearest neighbor-joining analysis is used when the company is interested in knowing which ones of their products are bestsellers in their branches.

For instance, if product A is a bestseller in Branch 1, and Branch 13 is where Product X is selling more, then it means that there is a high chance of Branch 2 selling as well considering that it is closer to

Branch 1 compared to Location 13 in response to product A than Product X.

Regression

When you are trying to establish the relationship between two variables, regression analysis is the way to go. With this technique, you can determine whether two variables are independent or dependent. Because of its predictive capabilities, this technique has gained so much popularity in the world of business. This explains the reason why it is often used in planning a business, marketing, budgeting, as well as forecasting the company's financial situation among other applications.

There are two variants of regressions, namely simple linear regression and multiple linear regression.

Simple Linear Regression

This one contains only one predictor, which is the independent variable, and one dependent variable, which results in a prediction. When you present it graphically, the regression model here demonstrates that there is a shorter distance or line between the Y- and the X-axis. Here, the X-axis is the predictor while the Y-axis is the prediction. In this case, simple linear regression is used for predictive purposes.

Multiple Linear Regression

This technique aims at predicting the values of response or prediction in relation to several independent variables or predictors.

When compared to simple regression, multiple linear regression is a little complex and labor-intensive, since you are handling large datasets.

Regression analysis is a technique used for the prediction of certain factors, for example, customer purchase behavior. For instance, you are trying to establish whether they use credit cards, cash or other modes of payments.

In the example we used previously, the company may choose to plan their repair and maintenance budget for equipment or they may determine that it is better to buy new equipment rather than plowing in so much money in the maintenance of an old one.

Decision Trees

One thing that makes this predictive technique quite popular is the fact that it provides a visual presentation of data values in a tree format. In the tree, you will see the original dataset which is further segmented into branches. The leaves represent the segments. The prediction here is a result of a wide range of decisions that are represented in a tree diagram in the form of Yes/No questions.

One of the questions that must be going through your mind is what makes this model more preferred by the users. Well, the truth is that many users find this model quite preferable because its segments come with descriptions. It is this versatility that offers you both predictive and descriptive value in a manner that is easy to understand. This explains why decision trees are gaining so much popularity and traction as far as data mining and database management.

Outlier Analysis

In an instance where models are already established or there is expected general behavior from a certain set of data objects, you may perform data mining by looking at outliers. Well, an outlier simply refers to a set of data objects that do not fall within an already established model. Alternatively, that which is not in compliance with the general behavior expected. The outcome of this variation may be data that one can use as a body of knowledge in the future.

A very good example of this is when you apply outlier analysis in detecting credit card fraud. On an online retailer story, you can get the shopping history of a specific client. This will tell you the behavior of the client in the market as far as their data goes.

When you are trying to establish whether there are fraudulent purchases made using the client's credit card, your focus should be to find out whether there are unusual purchases in their shopping history. For instance, you may look at whether there are unusually large amounts of money spent on a single purchase. You may also look for the unusual purchase of an item that is not related to their past shopping experience.

If, for the past three years, the client has made a purchase at least once in 2 months consistently, a single month where the client has purchased two or more times is enough to raise a red flag. It could mean that the client's credit card has been stolen or is being fraudulently used.

Evolution Analysis

If the data that you are trying to mine is inherently changing or evolving, you might want to establish a clear pattern that will play a significant role in predicting the future behavior of your dataset. In such a case, the recommended technique to employ is evolution analysis.

One thing that is important to note about evolution analysis is the fact that it involves identification, description and then modeling the trend patterns and other regularities to establish the behavior of your dataset. This way, you will find this being applied when mining and analyzing time-series data.

For instance, you may choose to use this when you are trying to look at the stock market trends as far as stock prices and the stock market, when subjected to a time-series analysis. This way, the outcome will go a long way in helping investors and stock market analysts to predict the future trend of the stock market. Ultimately, this will guide them when making stock investment decisions.

There are several other techniques you can employ when data mining and here, we have named those that are quite popular in their application. What is important to note is that when applying these techniques, you need to use several other tools and disciplines like software management, statistics, and mathematics, among others.

Note that the success of a business often rides on good management techniques when making important business decisions. One thing you should not forget that the quality of the decision you make is as good as the quality of information or knowledge you used when making them.

The truth is, when you use high-quality information, you will rely greatly on collecting, processing and evaluating the data. If the process of mining data was not successful or was less effective, this means that there is a high likelihood that the results will be a bag of knowledge that is not accurate and will not yield good business decisions.

Chapter 5

Association Rule Discovery

Well, in the previous chapter we have discussed various types of data mining techniques. In this chapter, we will discuss one of the descriptive data mining techniques - association rule discovery.

Well, you may be wondering what association rule discovery is all about. One thing you need to note about association rule discovery is that this is a procedure that is aimed at finding out frequent patterns, associations, correlations, and causal structures from datasets found in a wide range of databases. These databases include relational databases, transactional databases as well as data repositories.

When you have a set of transactions, the main role of the association rule mining is to find the rules that help in predicting the occurrence of specific items based on the occurrence of others in that very transaction.

Think of association rules as "if-then" statements that reveal the likelihood of a relationship between data items in a large dataset. There are so many applications of association rule widely used in discovering correlation in the medical dataset.

How Association Rule Discovery Works

At its basic level, association rule mining is all about machine learning, using ML models in the analysis of co-occurrence and patterns of data in the database. The aim is to identify frequently occurring "if-then" associations; these are then referred to as association rules.

There are two major parts of an association rule - antecedent (if) and the consequent (then). Well, the thing is that the antecedent is the item within the dataset while the consequent is the item that is found with it.

To create association rules, what is needed is to search the data for the frequent occurrence of "if-then" patterns and then using that criteria to support and offer confidence for the identification of the most relevant relationship. In this case, support implies how frequently an item appears in the data. However, confidence will also give us the number of times the if-then statements evaluate true. To compare the confidence of an item with the expected confidence, another metric, referred to as lift is used.

Therefore, what you need to bear in mind is that association rule discovery is all about calculating relationships from a set of at least two items. If the association rules are constructed from an analysis of all items in the itemset, the chances are that you will end up with so many rules that they hold little to no meaning at all. With that in mind, association rules are to be built from rules that are derived from a well-represented dataset.

Association Rule Algorithms

Some of the popular algorithms that use association rules include SETM, Apriori, AIS, and many other variations. With the SETM algorithm plays an important role in generating candidate itemsets while scanning through the database. However, the algorithm accounts for the itemsets once the scan is complete.

With the AIS algorithms, generation and counting of the itemsets are also done during the scanning of the data. When handling transaction data, it is the role of the AIS algorithm to determine which large itemset contained the specific transaction. This way, a new candidate itemset is then created by simply extending the large itemset along with other items in the transaction data.

In the case of SETM algorithms, the transaction ID and the candidate itemset are saved in a sequential structure. At the end of the pass, the support count for all the candidate itemsets is built by simply putting together the sequential structures.

One thing you will note about the AIS and the SETM algorithms is that they both create multiple candidate itemsets and count them as

Dr. Saed Sayad described in his publication, "Real-Time Data Mining".

On the other hand, the Apriori algorithm generates the candidate itemsets using only those that exceed the previous pass in size. In other words, the large itemset of the previous pass is added to itself so that all the itemsets generated after are one size larger. Any itemset that is generated but has a subset that is not large is deleted and what remains are treated as candidates.

It is important to note that with the Apriori algorithm, any subset of a frequent dataset is considered. This way, the algorithm lowers the number of candidates in consideration by simply exploring all item sets with a support count > minimum support count.

Use of Association Rules in Data Mining
One of the things you will note about association rule discovery in data mining is that it is used in conducting analysis or customers' behaviors and use that to predict other customer behaviors. In other words, they are commonly used in customer analytics, market basket analysis, catalog designs, product clustering as well as store layout.

Additionally, programmers often use association rule discovery when constructing programs that are capable of machine learning. Machine learning simply refers to a kind of artificial intelligence whose main aim is to build programs that are efficient and do not necessarily need to be programmed.

Let us take an example of association rule discovery in Market Basket Analysis (MBA). First, MBA is widely applied in grocery stores, telecommunications and banks among other business institutions. The results derived from this is what informs optimization of store layouts, plan coupon offers, designing product bundles, selecting the appropriate specials as well as choosing attached mailing in direct marketing.

In other words, the role of MBA is to help businesses understand what items have a high likelihood of being bought. For instance, people who purchase Toothpaste also are likely to buy a toothbrush, right? This means that the marketing teams at your retail store will probably target clients who buy toothpaste and toothbrush to give them an offer so that they can buy a third item like say mouthwash.

Now, if the clients buy toothpaste and toothbrush and then see a discount on mouthwash, the chances are that they will be encouraged to spend an extra shilling to get the mouthwash. And indeed, that is what market analysis is about!

Well, when you think of a transaction, what you are simply referring to is a single customer purchase. The items are things they purchase. Now, association discovery here is aimed at identifying items that are bought together in a specific event. In other words, the role of association rule discovery is to highlight frequent patterns of causal structures or associations among sets of items in the transaction database.

What you need to bear in mind is that the association discovery rules are based on the frequency counts of the number of items that occur alone and those that occur in combination based on the records in the database. In other words, you can say that if item X is part of an event, then item Y is likely to be part of the event too, at least Z% of the time. Hence, the association rule is the statement of an itemset X $\Rightarrow$ itemset Y.

In other words, if a customer buys a toothbrush, chances are that they will buy a toothpaste under the same transaction ID. What you need to understand here is that this is a co-occurrence pattern and not a causality one.

Now, the toothpaste example is just but a small subset of the business. If you take a real retail store that has thousands of items, chances are that you will make millions of revenue by simply making use of algorithms with the right item placements.

As we have already mentioned earlier, the association rule is composed of antecedent (A) and consequent (B), which can be represented as:

A => B

One thing you need to note is that either side of the association rule can have more than one item. The techniques employed here are borrowed from statistics and probability. The evaluation criteria in this case include support, confidence, and lift.

Support - simply refers to how frequently the combination happens in the market basket or in the database. Support refers to the % of baskets that contain items A and B of the association where the rule is true.

Support (A => B) = P (A ∩ B)

Expected confidence - simply refers to the probability of the consequent occurring if it were independent of the antecedent. In other words, the expected confidence will be the % of occurrence that contains B.

Expected confidence (A => B) = P (B)

Confidence - this simply refers to the strength of association between items, which is defined by the confidence factor. The confidence factor is the percentage of cases where the consequent appears when the antecedent has already occurred. In other words, confidence will be the percentage of baskets that have A and also contains B. that is, the % of baskets that contain B among those that contain A. (Confidence (A => B) ≠ Confidence (B => A))

Confidence (A => B) ≠ P (B\ A)

Lift - this is the confidence factor divided by the expected confidence. In other words, think of lift as a factor by which the probability of consequent rises given the antecedent. The expected confidence in this case refers to the number of consequent transactions divided by all transactions. Now, lift represents the ratio of the probability of you finding item X in the basket that has item Y, to the probability of finding X in any other random basket you select.

The good thing with MBA is that it is easy to understand, supports undirected data mining, and works on a wide range of data records using simple computations. Unfortunately, it often has an exponential increase in computations with quite a number of items.

Chapter 6

Decision Trees

In this chapter, we are going to expand more on the use of decision trees in data mining. A decision tree simply refers to a hierarchical relationship diagram that is often used in answering an overall question.

How does it do that?

Well, the way it achieves its goal is by first asking a sequence of sub-questions that are related to the main question. This means that every single branch of the tree represents a portion of a possible choice or response to a specific sub-question.

One thing that is important to note is that each sub-question iteratively lowers the number if remaining responses until you are left with one answer that is correct for the overall question.

Now, let us consider the following instance where the overall question is, "Is the weather good enough to go outside?"

Well, to say the truth, this is not a simple question to answer. This is mainly because there are so many factors that come in to play when it comes to determining what kind of weather is suitable to go outside or not. This means that, because you have so many options that you can choose from, you must create sub-questions, each of which has a possible response to it.

Here, we can have our first sub-question as, "is the weather windy?" You can respond with either Yes or No. Whatever your response is, you will have chosen the direction you would like to go in. Then this same response helps us create another sub-question, "what is the overall outlook?"

Again here, you can say that the outlook is sunny, rainy or overcast. With three different responses, you can choose to go towards one of the three directions. So, if it is sunny you will go, say left, if it is rainy you go right and if it is overcast, you go to the center.

The next sub-question would then be, "what is the humidity?" You think of the percentage of water in the atmosphere and in case that value is <80%, your response to the question would be a Yes! However, if the humidity is higher than 80%, the response to the overall question would be No!

But then you ask, "*How do Decision trees work*?"

One thing you need to note about decision trees is the fact that they fall under the family of supervised learning algorithms. Unlike other supervised learning algorithms, decision tree algorithms often play a significant role in solving classification and regression problems.

The main aim of the decision tree is to build a training model that can be used to predict a class of target variables. The best way to do this is to learn the decision tree rules that are inferred from prior training datasets.

The good thing is that the understanding level of decision tree algorithms is quite simple as opposed to other classification algorithms. The thing with the decision tree algorithms is that they solve problems by simply using tree representations. Each one of the internal nodes of the tree corresponds to a feature. On the other hand, the leaf nodes correspond to the class label.

What of The Decision Tree Algorithm Pseudocodes?

In this case, what you need to do is place the best attributes of the dataset at the root of the decision tree. Then proceed to split the training dataset into various subsets. You need to bear in mind that the creation of subsets should be done in such a manner that each one of the subsets contains data with the same values as the attributes. Finally, repeat what you have done on each of the subsets until you find a leaf node in all the branches of the tree.

When it comes to the prediction of class labels in decision trees, the most important thing is to ensure that you start from the roots of the tree. You simply compare the values of the root of the tree with the attributes in the record. Based on the comparison, you then choose to follow the branch that corresponds to the value before you jump onto the next node.

You then keep comparing the values of the attributes with the internal nodes of the tree to the point where you reach the leaf nodes with the predicted class values. As you may already know the manner in which the modeled decision tree is used in predicting the target class or value, the next important thing we need to understand is how to create the decision tree model itself.

Assumptions When Creating a Decision Tree

There are so many assumptions that one makes when building a decision tree. These assumptions include:

Assumption 1: at the very beginning, the entire training dataset is considered the root.

Assumption 2: it is important that the feature values are categorical. However, continuous values will be disconnected before you even think about building your model.

Assumption 3: Records are recursively distributed based on the attribute values.

Assumption 4: the sequence of placing attributes as an internal node or root of the tree is usually achieved using some statistical methods.

The other important point to note is that the decision trees follow the sum of the product (SOP) form of representation. If you are considering getting a job, the decision tree will help guide you on whether to consider the job offer or not. In other words, you can know whether to traverse the root node all the way to the leaf node.

The sum of the product representation is also referred to as the disjunctive normal form. This means that, for a class, every single branch from the root of the tree all the way to the leaf node of the tree with the same class is considered a conjunction/product of the values. However, if there are different branches that end in that class form, this is referred to as the disjunction sum.

One of the key challenges that one faces during the implementation of the decision tree is the fact that it is hard to identify which attributes need to be considered as the root node and which fall under other levels. Handling this is often referred to as the attribute selection. The good news is that there are several attribute selection measures that can help you identify what attributes to consider at each level of the root. Information gain and the Gini index are some of the most popular selection measures you can employ in this case.

Attributes Selection

If you have a dataset with n number of attributes, the first thing is for you to decide which ones of the attributes are going to be placed at the root of the tree, at internal nodes, or at other levels. This is not something simple. In fact, so many studies reveal that this is the most complicated step. When you randomly select any nodes to be the root, this cannot solve the issue. On the other hand, if we choose to follow the random approach, chances are that we will end up with bad results with a very low level of accuracy.

In order to resolve this attribute selection problem, researchers were able to come up with a method/approach that would address the issue. They simply suggested the use of some sort of criteria such as the Gini index or information gain to do that. The good thing with these criteria is that they will calculate values for every single attribute.

In this case, the values are sorted, and the attributes are positioned in the tree in ascending order with the highest value placed at the root of the decision tree. When using gain as the criteria, the assumption is that the attributes are categorical. On the other hand, when using the Gini index, the assumption here is that the attributes are continuous values.

Information Gain

When using the information gain as the criterion, it is important to try as much as possible to estimate the information contained by each one of the attributes. Here, we will use some information drawn from the information theory. If you want a measurement of how uncertain or random a variable Y is, you use entropy to define it.

If the problem is one of binary classification, you only have to consider either a positive or negative class. If, by chance, all the examples are positive or all of them are negative, then entropy is considered to be zero. However, if half of the records are said to be positive class while the other half are of the negative class, then the entropy value is one.

When you calculate the entropy value of the attributes, you get access to their information gain. The main role of information gain is to calculate the expected decline in entropy because of sorting the attributes.

Steps Involved in Building a Decision Tree

Step 1: Splitting

This simply refers to the partitioning of the data into smaller subsets. In such a case, specified variables are used for the split points. For instance, you can look at customers in a retail store and split them based on gender so that you can start doing targeted marketing campaigns and so on.

Step 2: Pruning

This refers to the shortening of the tree branches. In data mining, pruning refers to the process by which we reduce the tree size by turning branch nodes to leaf nodes and then removing the leaf nodes from beneath the original branch.

It is important to note that pruning is very useful considering that the classification tree may fit the training dataset but are likely to do a poor job when classifying new values. The simpler the tree, the less chance there is of overfitting.

That said, one thing that you need to bear in mind is that a decision tree classifier is simply a flowchart diagram with terminal nodes representing the classification decisions or outputs. When you start with a dataset, it is possible to measure entropy to determine ways of splitting the set until the point where all the data values fit into the same class.

So many approaches to decision trees exist, such as ID3, CART, and C4.5 among others. If you have nominal values, you can use the ID3 algorithm to split them. To visualize the tree data, it is important to use the Matplotlib library. Finally, understand that decision trees are prone to overfitting. This means that you have to prune the tree as much as possible to avoid overfitting. To do this, combine the adjacent nodes with low information gain and you are good to go.

Chapter 7

Data Integration

Well, when you think of the concept of data integration, it is pretty straightforward. This is because new information is simply merged with existing information. If you run a business that is regularly collecting information, then you know the essence of data integration.

One thing you need to note is that every business is concerned with accurate and up-to-date information. When you think about this critically, you will realize that data integration affects individuals too.

For instance, when you collect new phone numbers from a friend, add new music to your mobile device or when you receive a personal email among others. All these allow us to gain access to new information that you then merge with already existing information. One thing is for sure, all this information is transparent to us mainly because they happen behind the scenes.

One of the things that must be going through your mind is why data integration is a step in the process of data mining and why it is even useful. The truth is, we can only achieve faster processing of data, processing of complex queries, processing of high volumes of data as well as advanced data summarization among other functions by doing data integration. All these activities are crucial as far as data mining goes. It is through data integration that we are able to identify patterns and establish a correlation between items in the database that will inform future trends.

Understanding Data Integration in the Real World

To get a good sense of what data integration is all about, let us consider a company that is a leader in local advertising and information. The company seeks to offer agile analytics solutions to its commercial team to help them in making the right decisions in the wake of digital transformation. In such a case, the company chooses to go with Connect for Big data.

This allows the company to not only extract and transform data but also load data from a wide range of sources into Hadoop. According to the individual charged with the responsibility of business intelligence in the company, connect for big data is one of the most robust solutions both in terms of speed and volume. This is exactly what the company needs to respond to new business needs in an ever-evolving world of digital transformation.

With Connect for Big data, the company will be managing several terabytes of data. In fact, they can access information in real-time.

They can now refresh data based on product segments, agency as well as the geographical location of the store. In other words, you can bring data from a wide range of sources to inform the decision-making process. The other benefit is the fact that the data will help the company achieve ROI within a duration of three years of getting Connect for Big Data.

That said, incorporating data integration in data mining goes a long way in helping businesses derive more and more value from the available information. With this capacity, better decision making becomes the order of the day.

Issues Associated with the Process of Data Integration and Their Solutions

Data integration like any other field is not without challenges. One of the most complicated issues associated with data integration is associated with setting up a more pragmatic prospect. During the requirement analysis stage, you can easily pick out all the issues that are associated with data integration.

These complications include:

- Lack of manpower

- Varied information

- Awful information

- Shortage of storeroom competence

Lack of Manpower

With every passing day, data integration is expanding, and its applications are significantly increasing. However, one of the challenges that still remain is the fact that there is limited manpower. In other words, the number of people who are skilled is not adequate enough to meet the high demands of the industry.

One thing that is important to bring into perspective when you think of this is the fact that every project is accompanied by its own problems and requirements for skilled manpower that can help resolve a number of issues associated with data integration. With the advent of advanced databases, there is a need for data in the old databases to be moved into newly built databases. In this case, a high budget is needed, the lack of which becomes a stumbling block for efficient data transfers.

To address this issue, expert data managers as well as experienced project leaders are required to take care of the data integration process and ensure that they have all required skill sets. The only way to ensure that we have a modular and robust environment for improved data integration and efficient data transfer is to ensure that we select the best candidates for the job. These candidates need to have true practical experience and Skillset in the industry.

Varied Information

During data integration, there is co-ordination of large volumes of information from inherent systems. These inherent systems are produced from databases that are hierarchical in nature. One thing you will note is that their production is quite distinct from conventional databases. This is mainly because the inherent databases keep adding new data to increase its value over time. Here, there are various strategies one can employ when copying heterogeneous data.

To address this issue, a data warehouse is chosen to serve as an environment that meets the needs of a wide range of business services while also helping in the utilization of data. The format of the data is then standardized so that it can be used by any application.

Additionally, collecting data from a wide range of databases and then adding that up in one database can be quite tender. This is a very challenging task, but the good thing is that technology has reached its peak and allows query languages to gain access to almost all types of advanced and traditional databases.

Poor Information

When you are performing data mining for analysis, it is important that you are gathering high-quality data. Otherwise, poor quality data will affect the data integration process severely. The truth is that most databases face serious problems because the kinds of data they hold have impure features.

Therefore, to have good quality data integration, ensure that the data you are adding into the database is good quality data. If not, then it is critical that integration is investigated over and over again to ensure that it has no effect on the ultimate quality of information derived.

The most important thing is to ensure that from the very beginning, practices and tests are performed to ascertain the quality of data so that the whole process of data integration is flawless. It is the responsibility of the users and the quality controllers to ensure that they work together hand in hand to clear any questionable faults the end-users might face so that the process of data integration is enhanced.

Shortage of Storeroom Competence

One of the major challenges businesses face during data integration is the lack of storage. If you do not have enough space to store your data, then this makes it difficult for businesses to offer scalability and elasticity for their data. This means that the growth of data stops. Additionally, seeing to it that a larger architecture is added is a big deal as this would be even more expensive.

Here, the best thing to do is to seek alternate solutions for storage in data warehouses. The good thing is that the enhancement of science and technology has made storage less costly. In fact, according to statistics, the cost is thought to have reduced at least ten times over the last four years.

Insights of Data Integration as an Irresistible Attempt

If you are going to analyze data and meet the infrastructure needs, there are two major factors that have to come into play - capital and skilled manpower. If your company lacks enough capital and manpower, it will be in so much pressure which makes it hard for the company to move forward, meet their objectives and solve their client's problems.

Therefore, it is critical that systematic preparations be done in the process of data integration. It is critical that proper planning is done to ensure that targets are met. To do this, the processes have to be more elastic to help companies overcome risks and doubts. Rather than concentrating on bigger targets, the best option is to focus on achieving smaller targets first, which you can achieve by doing them one step at a time. This way, the tasks become easier and simpler with time.

Chapter 8

Data Transformation

Data transformation refers to the process of converting data from one structure/format to another. Just like data integration, data transformation is very important when it comes to data mining. One thing that is important to note is that data transformation is a long process that involves a wide range of activities. These activities include conversion of data types, cleaning of data by getting rid of nulls and duplicate values, data enrichment, aggregation, among others depending on the project needs.

Typically, data transformation is a two-stage process.

Stage 1
This involves the performance of data discovery. This simply means the identification of various sources of data and data types.

The next thing in this stage if the determination of the data structure and the kind of data transformation that needs to happen.

Finally, performing data mapping, which is central to defining how various fields in the data are mapped, modified, joined together, filtered out, and aggregated.

Stage 2

Here, you begin by extracting data from the original source. It is important to bear in mind that the sources of data often vary and can be structured (e.g. databases), streaming sources (e.g. telemetry from connected devices), or log files that are derived from customers that use the web applications.

The next thing in this stage is to perform transformation itself. Here, what you need to do is transform the data by aggregating say the sales data or converting their formats, joining the columns and rows, or even editing the text strings.

Finally, you send the transformed data to the target stores. Ensure that the target is the database or a data warehouse that is responsible for handling structured as well as unstructured datasets.

Why Transform Data?

This is one of the most important questions that many people ask. Well, the truth is that data transformation is often performed for a number of reasons. From a general point of view, businesses often transform their data to ensure that they are compatible with other data. They also transform the data before moving them to another system, joining them with other datasets, or even aggregating information in the data.

Let's consider a scenario where your company has acquired a smaller company. The point is that you need to combine the human resource department information for both companies. However, the company that you have just bought uses a different database from the parent company. This means that you will need to do some work to ensure that the records from both companies match.

Now, each of the new employees has an employee ID which you can use to serve as a primary key. However, the other thing you need to change is the way in which the dates have been formatted. It is also important that duplicate rows are eliminated. The other thing is to ensure that you do not have null values on the Employee ID field, so that every employee in the companies are accounted for.

All these activities are to be performed in a staging area prior to loading up the data to the final target. That said, there are many other reasons why data transformation is important. For instance, if you are moving your data to a new location such as a cloud data warehouse, then you might want to change the data types.

Alternatively, you might want to join streaming data or unstructured data with structured data to allow you to analyze the whole dataset together. You may also want to add information to your dataset for the purposes of enrichment. Therefore, you may do data enrichment, the addition of timestamps, or the addition of geolocation data. The other reason is that you might want to perform aggregation of data by first comparing the sales data from a wide range of regions or totaling the sales from all the locations the company has stored.

How is Data Transformed?

There are various methods that are employed during data transformation. These methods include:

Scripting

This simply means that you perform data transformation using scripts like Python or SQL among others. In other words, you simply write a code that will help you extract the data you want and then transform that particular dataset.

Cloud-Based ETL Tools

One thing to bear in mind is that the ETL (Extract, Transform, Load) tools are hosted in the cloud. This means that you have to leverage the expertise and infrastructure of the vendor to transform the data.

On-Premise ETL Tools

It is important to note that ETL tools often take much of the stress out of scripting transformations by simply automating the whole process. These ETL tools are simply those that are hosted within the company's site and often need extensive expertise as well as infrastructure costs.

What are Some of the Data Transformation Challenges?

There are a number of difficulties that are associated with data transformation. These include:

Time Constraint

The truth is that when performing data transformation, you may need to clean the data before transforming it or moving it to another location. This is something that can be time-consuming and is a complaint that is common among data scientists working with unstructured data.

High Cost

Based on the kind of infrastructure your company has in place, the transformation of data may require a team of experts and a huge cost of infrastructure.

Slow Process

The process of data transformation can be very slow. This is because extracting and transforming data can be a huge burden on the system. in most cases, this is done in small batches. This simply means that you take up to 24 hours before you start running the next batch and if you have several batches, it can take weeks or even months to have all the data extracted and transformed. The truth is that this takes a lot of time in making important business decisions.

Data Transformation Techniques

Well, when it comes to data transformation, the routine is that you convert the data into a suitable format that can be mined. Some of the methods that you can employ in data transformation include:

Smoothing

This process simply uses binning, clustering and regression analysis of the data to eliminate noise from the dataset.

Attribute Construction

In this section, what you need to do is construct new attributes before adding them to a given set of attributes that already exist in *the database.*

Aggregation

This simply entails the performance of operations on the dataset.

Concept Hierarchy Generation for Nominal Data

In this case, the attributes are generalized to a higher concept level.

Normalization

In this case, the attribute data is often scaled as much as possible to ensure that they fall within a smaller range. One thing that you need to note is that data has to be normalized to avoid dependency on the choice of measurement units used on the data attributes.

In other words, you are transforming or mapping the data to a common or smaller range. In such a case, all the data attributes become equal weight after the process. There are several normalization methods that can be used. These include:

Min-Max Normalization

The main role of this form of normalization is to ensure that the relationship among the original data values is preserved and a linear transformation is done of that original dataset. This means that the applicable ones of the actual minimum and maximum values of the attributes are normalized.

Normalization by Decimal Scaling

The process of normalization here simply involves moving the decimal point of the values of the attributes.

Z-Score Normalization

In this case, the values of an attribute are simply normalized on the bases of the mean and standard deviation of the attributes. Note that this is useful when the actual maximum and minimum values of the attributes are not known in the first instance.

Discretization

In this case, the raw values of the numeric attributes are often replaced by conceptual labels or even interval labels as part of the whole discretization routine. In other words, the numeric values are transformed by simply mapping them to interval or concept labels. To achieve this, you can employ a number of techniques:

Binning

This is nothing more than a splitting technique, unsupervised, and based on a series of bins.

Cluster Analysis

In this case, you need to apply a clustering algorithm in order to discretize the numerical attributes. This is done by first partitioning the values of these attributes into groups or clusters.

Histogram Analysis

The role of the histogram here is to partition the attribute's values into disjoint ranges, otherwise referred to as bins or buckets. This is also an example of an unsupervised method.

Decision Tree Analysis

In this case, the use of the decision tree employs the approach of top-down splitting. As a supervised method, this involves the selection of values of attributes with a minimum entropy to serve as a split-point in order to discretize them. Additionally, the values are then recursively partitioned such that the resulting intervals arrive at a hierarchical discretization.

Correlation Analysis

This simply employs the bottom-up approach by seeking out the best neighboring interval which is then merged to form a larger interval recursively. Just like decision tree analysis, this is also a supervised method.

Data transformation best practices

Start with the End in Mind

In this case, all you are doing is designing the target. It is important to note that when you are faced with lots of data to process, most of the people are tempted to jump right into the nuts and bolts of data transformations. However, prior to transforming your dataset into insights that can be used in making decisions, it is critical that you engage business users. This plays a role in helping you understand the business processes that you are trying to analyze so that you can effectively design the target.

This process is often referred to as dimensional modeling. It results in two major types of target tables for the transformed data:

Fact Tables

This is important in storing the events under measurement and then attempts to answer the "how many" questions. Some of the types of fact tables include transaction, periodic snapshot as well as accumulating snapshot. The transaction tables keep records of events at the finer or atomic level. The periodic snapshot is responsible for summarizing events over a given duration of time. Finally, the accumulating snapshot is responsible for capturing the process of execution, the steps of which often occur at regular intervals within one record.

Dimensional Tables

This kind of table is responsible for providing all the nitty-gritty details of the data. According to the data warehousing guru, Ralph Kimball, the dimension tables are the data warehouse's core. This is mainly because the dimension tables contain entry points as well as detailed labels that allow the system to be used for the sake of business analytics.

One thing that you need to note here is that dimensional modeling often targets the users for the sake of:

- Engaging the users early enough so that they have a kind of control over the outcome.

- The scope of the data transformation efforts is identified by the data alone for the sake of fulfilling the needs of its users

- Providing the star schema fact table relationship in such a way that the dimensions are quite easy for the users to understand.

- Offers targets for the efforts of data transformation

Speeding the Date of the Data with Data Profiling

Here, the most important thing you need to understand is that you need to have knowledge of the data you are trying to analyze as this highlights the data sources for transformation. For instance, if you seek to analyze the sales trends, it is critical that you access the client database as well as the product database. This way, you can pull in the results of the sales from a POS (point-of-sale system). When you pinpoint the source, the raw data can be extracted into a usable format.

Before you hop into data transformation, the first thing you need to do is perform data profiling so you can better understand the exact state of the raw data. This will also help you know how much work is needed so the data can be analyzed.

In other words, the purpose of profiling the data is to help you know your data well prior to transformation. It is critical that you know the size of your dataset, the heads of the columns, the data type in each column, the relationship between the columns, the range of values in every column, the number of rows, as well as how many missing values there are, and how often poor data shows up.

Cleaning the Data

Now that you are armed with deeper insights from the data profiling, you can see just what is involved and the kind of transformation needed to do on your dataset for it to be usable.

For instance, if the source data field is the format YYYY/MM/DD and the target data field is in MM-DD-YYYY format, the source fields need to be transformed so that they match with the required format. On the other hand, if there are some columns that show a lot of missing values or poor data, it is critical that you have a conversation with the business stakeholders so that you can determine whether the missing values should be estimated or discarded.

Understand that cleaning your data in the early stages of transformation goes a long way in ensuring that bad data will not get to the end-user. This gives business owners complete confidence that the data will produce the best results.

Conform the Data

Now, the last three practices that we have discussed simply set the stage for the transformation of data into a target format. This is also referred to as data conformation. In this case, the data transformation team is aware of the source and this ensures that they can meet the user's needs as far as the data attributes go, to help in the analysis of the business process.

Here, the first thing to do is to map the source columns to the target columns. In this case, ETL tools are used in the automation of the data flow in all columns on succeeding data loads.

One major benefit you can draw from using this kind of data is that the silos between the data can easily be broken down using business intelligence. Note that the siloed data, in between a wide range of data stores often requires lots of work when merging them so that they create a meaningful analysis. Additionally, conformed data often requires little pre-processing while freeing up analysts for the addition of value to the data.

Build Dimensions and Then Facts

As we have already discussed in the previous sections, using dimensions helps in putting context around the data. On the other hand, the role of the facts is to explain what truly happened within the dimensional context. For instance, products, customers, and dates could serve as dimensions. The sales results and the measures serve as the facts in this case.

But then why would you load dimensional tables first?

One major advantage of loading the dimensional tables first is so these newly loaded fact records can link to a more meaningful dimensional record. The truth is that sales data could not be meaningful if the link to date, product and customer dimensions do not exist. Therefore, it is important to ensure that the date, product and customer dimensions are kept up-to-date with every data load and then followed by the fact tables from the sales.

Considering the stakeholder engagements performed before the transformation of the data, what is interesting to discover is the need to create special fact tables of common aggregates. This goes a long way in saving the users time during data analysis. Here, the accumulating and periodic snapshots we discussed previously come in to play. That is, you can pre-aggregate the sales volumes by the product and quarter/month/week.

Record Audit and Data Quality Events

During data transformation, the most beneficial thing to do is track audits and the data quality metrics. This is mainly because audit tracking goes a long way in capturing the number of records loaded at each step of the data transformation process. It also considers the time at which every step took place. Some of the data quality tests include a follow up of the screen types performed on inbound data.

The other important question you need to ask is whether the columns include junk, null data or out-bound values.

The structures of the data often play an important role in testing the relationship between the tables and columns. For instance, do all the sales fact records connect back to valid customer records?

The business rule also is concerned with checking the sanity of the entire dataset. For instance, you may want to know whether the current data loads sales volume reveals a statistically valid variation from a previous data load.

Capturing the data quality test results, including them in the audit records for the data loads, and then linking back the fact records to the audit records offers the ability to reconstruct the lineage of the facts data. It also helps a great deal in proving the validity of the metrics calculated using the fact data.

Using an approach like this, analysts can work backward, answering the question, "where did this data originate from?" and, "how can we know we have the right metrics?" – two questions business stakeholders ask frequently.

Having the right answers to these questions can give business users the confidence they need in the newly transformed dataset. Plus, it means the team responsible for transforming the data has a base to work from in future user engagement.

Continually Engaging the User Community

As far as data transformation goes, the very best value measurement lies in how the target users agree with and continually makes use of the transformed datasets. This means that the end of your data transformation process is not the point where you make sure the end-users have ready access to the conformed data.

What you need to understand is that this is only the beginning of the process.

The truth is that transformed data has to go through stringent testing to ensure it is usable. It is the data teams' responsibility to address all defects found by the business users in real-time use.

For most businesses, the current data proliferation is akin to being a gold mine that they can tap into. However, as it is with gold, this kind of data has to extracted very carefully, assessed, refined, and then delivered, otherwise its value is meaningless. When you understand the data transformation fundamentals, you can start to realize valuable business insights from this data which, in turn, can have a positive impact on business decisions.

Chapter 9

Data Warehousing

———◆———

Data warehousing is very important when it comes to data mining. It is through data warehousing that a data warehouse is built and used. A data warehouse is often built by integrating data from a wide range of sources that offer support to analytical reporting, decision making as well as ad hoc and structured queries. Data warehousing comprises such activities as data cleaning, consolidation and integration.

Do you have a database in your company? Well, if you do then you know the content, right?

Well, the truth is that a database is made up of at least one file, usually many more, that must be stored, either on a computer or some other storage device. In bigger organizations, you will notice that databases are not kept on employee computers. Instead, they are stored in a central system that typically consists of several computer servers.

What is a server? Well, a server simply refers to a computer system that offers service over a specific network. It is often located in a secured room, only accessible by authorized persons. Typically, one thing you will note is that the database files reside inside the service but you can access them remotely from a number of computers in the company. As the number of these databases grow and become more complex, we stop referring to them as ordinary databases and start calling them data warehouses.

Therefore, you can think of a data warehouse as multiple databases put together to achieve a specific function. It is through a data warehouse that data integration from a wide range of databases is made possible. This is what offers insight into the data. The ultimate objective of a database is not just the storage of data, but also inform the business decision-making process based on what the data says.

One thing that you have to note about a data warehouse is that it offers support to this objective by offering a range of tools and architecture that systematically organizes and understands data from a number of databases.

Data Warehouse Types

There are three major types of data warehouses, namely:

Information Processing

A data warehouse plays an important role in processing all stored data. This data in the storage can be processed by several means such as querying, basic statistical analysis, as well as reporting using charts, tables, graphs, and crosstabs among others.

Data Mining

This supports the knowledge discovery process that is aimed at seeking out any hidden patterns and associations, performing classifications, constructing analytical models as well as doing predictions. The results of the mining process can then be presented using a wide range of visualization tools.

Analytical Processing

The other part of data warehousing is to support the analytical processing of information that is in storage. The analysis of data in this case can be achieved using OLAP operations, such as drill up, slice-and-dice, pivoting, and drill down among others.

Using Data Warehouse Information

Today, there are many decision support technologies that have been developed to help in the utilization of available data in the data warehouse. It is with the help of these technologies that executives can effectively and quickly use the data warehouses when they are mining data. In other words, the business executives can gather, analyze and make decisions based on the information they derive from the data in the warehouse.

The information you derive from the data warehouse can be used for the following:

Customer Analysis

This is often done by analyzing the buying preferences of a client, their buying time as well as budget cycle, among others.

Tuning Production Strategies

One thing that is important to bear in mind when tuning the product strategies is that you can reposition the products and manage product portfolios by comparing the annual or quarterly sales.

Operations Analysis

It is important to note that data warehousing plays a significant role when it comes to the management of customer relationships as well as making environmental corrections. The information also goes a long way in conducting business operations analysis.

How to Integrate Heterogeneous Databases

There are two major approaches that go a long way in integrating heterogeneous databases. These approaches include:

Update-Driven Approach

Well, this is an alternative to the traditional query-driven approach we have just discussed. Today's data warehouse systems follow an update-driven approach instead of the traditional method. In this approach, the information that you derive from the multiple heterogeneous sources is integrated in advance and then stored in a warehouse. The good thing is that this kind of information is available for both direct querying and analysis.

One of the advantages of using this approach is the fact that it offers high performance. The data in the semantic data store undergoes copying, processing, integration, annotation, summarization, and then restructuring in advance. Finally, there is no requirement for an interface at the local sources for data to be processed.

Query-Driven Approach

It is important to note that the query-driven approach is a rather traditional method used in the integration of heterogeneous databases. The main aim of building this approach was to create integrators and wrappers at the top of a wide range of heterogeneous databases. These integrators are often referred to as mediators.

To start the integration process using this approach the very first thing that you need to do is check when the client issues a query. The query is translated by the metadata dictionary into a suitable format that matches the individual heterogeneous sites involved. After this, the queries get mapped and forwarded onto the local query processor. Finally, the outcome from the heterogeneous sites gets added to a global response set.

There are a number of disadvantages associated with the query-driven approach. Some of these disadvantages include:

- This often requires a complex process, involving filtering and integration process

- It is not very efficient

- If you are dealing with frequent queries, this approach can be very costly

- Additionally, if the queries you are handling require aggregations, the query-driven approach can also be very expensive.

Data Warehouse Tools and Utility Functions

The data warehouse is important in:

- Data extraction, which is the gathering of data from a wide range of heterogeneous sources

- Data cleaning, which means to locate and fix mistakes and errors in the data

- Data transformation, which means to convert the data from the existing format to the format that is used in the warehouse

- Data loading, which involves the sorting, summarizing, consolidation, integrity checking, as well as constructing indices and finally partitioning them.

- Refreshing, which involves ensuring that the data is updated from the source to the warehouse.

That said, one thing you will note about operational databases is that as they grow bigger, they become more complex to keep them in a single location. The storage capacity becomes a big issue as well as performance and security factors. This means that you have to consider a company that has several offices across the globe.

The truth is that you can create one large database at the main office and then have all subsidiary offices connect to this database. However, what is important to note is that each time an employee tries to connect to work with the database, they will be required to create a connection over several thousands of miles via hundreds of network nodes. If you are moving a relatively smaller amount of data, this will not present a major challenge.

What happens if you are handling a large database? In such a case, it may not be efficient to move large amounts of data across the network. In this case, the best option is to have a distributed database. In other words, the database has multiple, interrelated databases that are stored in different locations on the computer network.

If you are a typical user, this distributed database has to be centralized. However, behind the scenes, parts of this database are located in different locations. The typical features of a distributed database management system include:

- Multiple network sites connected via a communication system,

- Availability of data at any site to users in other sites

- The data at each site is under the control of the database management system (DBMS)

The chances are that you have already used a distributed database without really knowing it. For instance, you may have an email account from one of the major service providers like Gmail or yahoo. Where do you think your emails reside? The truth is that the company that is hosting your email account utilizes a wide range of locations without you having the knowledge of it.

One of the major advantages of using a distributed database is that data access and processing is fast. On the other hand, the major disadvantage here is that associated with the complexity of management. The truth is that setting up a distributed database is the role of the database administrator who has specialized database management skills.

That said, it is critical to be aware of the fact that operational databases undergo changes frequently based on the number of transactions that happen within the account. Supposing you are a business executive and you would like to analyze the feedback of any data like the consumer data, product data or even the supplier data. At this point, you will not have any data to analyze because the previous data has been updated in light of new transactions.

With a data warehouse, you have access to more generalized and consolidated data in a multi-dimensional view. In addition to the generalized and consolidated view of the data, it is also the role of the data warehouse to offer access to Online Analytical Processing

(OLAP) tools that are important during data mining. It is these tools that play an important role in helping us perform interactive and effective data analysis in a multi-dimensional space. It is this kind of data analysis that gives rise to data generalization and data mining.

The data mining functions, like clustering, association, classification, and prediction, can be integrated with the OLAP operations for the sake of enhancing interactive knowledge mining at different abstraction levels. This explains the reason why the data warehouse is gaining in popularity as an important data analysis platform and online analytical data processing.

Why is a Data Warehouse Separated from Operational Databases?

Data warehouses and operational databases are separated for several reasons:

An operational database is built for common tasks and workloads. These include indexing and searching for specific records among others. On the other hand, the data warehouse queries are known for their complexity and the fact that they present a more generalized form of the data.

An operational database offers support to the parallel processing of several transactions. This means that there is a need for adequate mechanisms to control and recover operational databases; this ensures the database is efficient, consistent and robust.

Operational database queries often permit reading and modification of operations. OLAP on the other hand requires read-only access to stored data.

Finally, operational databases are known to maintain data that exists now, while the role of the data warehouse is for the maintenance of historical data.

Features of a Data Warehouse

Some of the features of a data warehouse include:

Subject-Oriented

The reason why the data warehouse is said to be subject oriented is mainly that it offers information around the subject instead of the ongoing operations within an organization. These subjects often range from suppliers, customers, products, revenue and sales among others. The truth is that the data warehouse doesn't focus on ongoing company operations. Instead, they focus on the analysis and modeling of data for the sake of informing the decision-making process.

Integrated

One thing you need to note about the data warehouse is that it is built by simply integrating data from a wide range of heterogeneous sources like relational databases and flat files among others. It is this kind of integration that plays a significant role in enhancing the effective analysis of data.

Non-Volatile

The term, non-volatile, points at the previous data not erased when the new set of data is added into the system. One thing you need to understand is that the data warehouse and the operational databases are segregated. This means that when there are frequent changes in the operational database, they are not mirrored in the data warehouse.

Time-Variant

The other thing to note is that the data collected in the data warehouse is often identified within a certain time frame. This is mainly because the data in the data warehouse offers access to information derived from a historical perspective.

That said, you have to note that the data warehouse does not necessarily need processing of transactions, concurrency control or even recovery of transactions. This is mainly because the data is stored in a physical format, separated from the operational database.

Applications of the Data Warehouse

As we have already discussed, a data warehouse is charged with the responsibility of helping business executives to organize and analyze data so that the information drawn from the analysis informs the decision-making process. In other words, the data warehouse serves as the sole part of the plan-execute-evaluate feedback system for the purpose of enterprise management.

Their application is evident in such fields as:

- Financial services

- Consumer goods

- Banking services

- Controlled manufacturing

- Retail sectors

Key takeaways

- A data warehouse is indeed a database that is distinct from the company's operational database

- There is no need for frequent updating in the data warehouse

- Data warehousing is concerned with processing historical data that plays an important role in helping the company analyze its business model

- A data warehouse supports business executive in organizing, understanding and utilizing their data in making strategic decisions

- The data warehouse system plays a significant role in the diverse integration of application systems

- Data warehouse systems go a long way in consolidating historical data analysis

Chapter 10

Data Mining Challenges

The state of data mining is not without its challenges. Most organizations today, irrespective of shape and size, have their attention focused on in-depth analysis of their data so that they can use the information derived thereof to perfect their future investments and customer experience.

One thing you will note in this time and age is that the amount of data we store and analyze is rapidly expanding. Based on recent statistics, Google gets more than 20 million search queries every minute. Over the same span of time, 200M emails are being sent and 48hours of video exchanged on YouTube. We have not even mentioned the number of Tweets, Instagram and Facebook messages among other social media platforms.

When you add all this data, along with other mediums like platforms for trading stocks and new platforms, you generate millions of data exchanges every minute. What is interesting is the fact that not so long ago, a wide range of companies began to collect and store data and, in terms of research and analysis, that puts them ahead of the game.

In spite of the fact that data mining is an incredibly powerful system for collecting data, there are so many challenges it faces, for and during the implementation process; challenges related to the mining methods, performance and data collection among others.

It is critical that these problems are resolved. Some of these problems include:

- Poor quality data collected. This is one of the biggest and most common challenges associated with data mining. This comes in the form of noisy data, misplaced datasets/values, dirty data, not enough data, incorrect values, and poor representation of the study population during the collection process, among others.

- There is also data redundancy during the integration process. This often is something that happens from a wide range of unmasked sources. The data can be in a number of from such as social interaction data, numerical data, media files, and geo-location data among others.

- Security and privacy issues. This is a big deal that needs to be taken seriously. The main reason why this is a huge problem is the fact that it gradually increases for every data mining company. Looking at the concerns from private, public and governmental organizations, this is one of the genuine ones that threaten the safety and privacy of protected data.

- Data that exceeds its static boundaries. This is something that is both cost-sensitive and unbalanced. This often is the case when there are consistent updates in data collection models aimed at analyzing the velocity of data and any other updated incoming dataset.

- The difficulty of access and data unavailability. This is one of the biggest concerns that is faced by a wide range of companies in different sectors. So many factors that are hard to calculate and organize comes in to play, slowing down the process.

- Structuring large quantities of unstructured data. The problems come in when there is a huge amount of data counts hence creating a real issue when it comes to trying to organize them into a more structured format. The challenges come in so many forms, namely manpower, financial outputs, and time constraint among others. This similar issue often arises when there are enormous amounts of output from a wide range of data mining methods under the collection.

- Issues related to cost also arise. This is because of the high cost associated with the software needed for data collection, not to mention the required hardware, used in accumulating and organizing huge piles of data from a wide range of sectors. For companies that collect data, this translates to a significant financial challenge they can ever face as far as data is concerned.

We have already seen what these challenges are, and it is high time we shed more light on the common issues. While some challenges aren't experienced as widely compared to others, it is critical that we understand and assess solutions for them.

Noisy Data

Did you know that the process of data mining involves information derived from a large volume of data? Well, the truth is that the real-world data we collect is 'noisy', diverse and unstructured. In most cases, such kind of data can be quite unreliable.

Most of these challenges arise as a result of measurement errors and quantification by faulty instruments as well as human error.

Let us consider an example to further provide insight into the problem. Supposing there is a retail store that collects customer email IDs for all their purchases. Then at one point, they decide to segment their clients into groups of those with high purchases in the store and those with low purchases. This is so that they can send them exclusive offers and discounts.

What do you think will happen?

One thing you will realize is that the kind of data they have is flawed. There are so many clients who would have given their information with spelling mistakes or entered the wrong email address. There are those that might have even entered the wrong email address just for privacy concerns. This is exactly what we mean by 'noisy' data.

Distributed/Scattered Data

The real-world data is, in most cases, stored in a wide range of mediums. This could be the internet or any other protected database. In order to collate the data into one structure is something that is very beneficial as far as achieving data mining goals. However, one thing you need to bear in mind is that lots of data contain lots of speed bumps.

For instance, if a corporation owns many offices in many locations, they are likely to have data saved many other locations on their protected server/database. This means that, to mine such kind of data requires skilled manpower, the use of algorithms, and sophisticated tools that pertain to that very location.

Complex Data Restructuring

One thing you need to bear in mind is that the data that exists out there in the real world assumes varied forms. There is data in numeric form, text form, audio form, graphical form, and video form among others. To extract information from this kind of data and then compile them into consumable information from a diverse and heterogeneous medium can be a complex process.

Algorithm Performance

The use of algorithms is one of the most essential areas of data mining. This is because the performance of data mining processes can be ultimately based on the method and algorithm used during mining. If these algorithms and methods are not accurate and up to the mark for the assigned task, the outcome will not be needed and hence affecting the end data. This is will in turn affect the complete campaign.

Incorporating Background Knowledge

If you are going to do data mining properly, then you need adequate background knowledge in the process. It is through background knowledge that the end outcome of the process achieves a high degree of accuracy, explaining the reason why it is so essential.

One thing to note about background knowledge is the fact that predictive tasks can become actual predictions while descriptive tasks give accurate results. That said, the collection and implementation of background knowledge is something that is both difficult and time-consuming for most data mining organizations.

Data Protection, Data Privacy

One issue that is common among individuals, public and private organizations is how they can protect the privacy of their data. The field of data mining and the operations involved often invoke a wide range of issues surrounding the protection and security of the data.

A very good example of this would be a retailer that makes a note of the products every time a customer orders groceries. When you look at this kind of data, it implies what the client's interest is in a wide range of products. This is one of the reasons why so many data mining companies across the globe integrate strong security measures to protect the data they collect from their clients so that they are not misused by parties with hidden agendas.

Data Mining Trends

As the days pass by, data mining is evolving into an important tool for most organizations in the world. This is the more reason to progress and come up with solutions to all the challenges we have discussed above. Note that some of the largest businesses in the world make use of data mining techniques to decrease costs, drive sales, increase revenue and identify new clients.

Additionally, organizations are leveraging new definitive guides like this one to learn trends in data mining. One of the best examples here is the price-check app for Amazon. You can use this app for scanning products, finding prices in-store through text messages, and performing product searches, among others. This way, the companies are able to collect intelligence information pertaining to clients, products and their competitors.

Another very good example is Delta, a cross-platform data mining company. One thing the airline does is consistently keep an eye on complaints they get through their online platforms, like Twitter. When they get tweets that have issues, the airlines resolve these issues almost instantly. These issues can be related to baggage. This way, the airline provides customer satisfaction and gains important customer data, among other factors, that improve their client experience.

These are just but a few examples of how companies are using data mining to improve their operations. One thing is for sure, data mining challenges organizations face can take time to resolve. However, the thing is that once they are addressed, that becomes a game-changer for the company earning them profits that grows the company.

Chapter 11

Data Mining Tools

There are many data mining tools available in the market. However, I have put together the most commonly used ones that will surely give you a great experience. Come with me:

Rapid Miner

This is an open-source tool. One thing you will note about Rapid Miner is that it is one of the very best predictive analysis systems develop by a company referred to as Rapid Miner and is written in JAVA programming language. It is important to note that this tool offers an integrated environment for deep learning, machine learning, text mining as well as predictive analysis.

You can use this tool for a wide range of applications such as commercial applications, business applications, research, application development, training, education, and machine learning among others.

The other thing with Rapid miner is that it offers the serves as a private/public cloud as well as a premise infrastructure. It has a client/server model that is used as its base. It also comes with a template-based framework that allows for the speedy delivery of work with a minimal number of errors, commonly expected in the manual code process of writing.

It comes with three major modules:

- Rapid Miner Studio - which plays a significant role in workflow design, validation, prototyping among others.

- Rapid Miner Server - this plays a significant role as a predictive data model that is created in the studio.

- Rapid Miner Radoop - this plays a key role in directly executing processes in the Hadoop cluster for simplification of predictive analysis.

Orange

Just like Rapid miner, Orange is also an open-source data mining tool. One thing with Orange is that it is perfect for both data mining and machine learning. It plays a significant role in data visualization and is a component-based software. Orange has been written in Python programming language.

Considering that this is a component-based software, its components are referred to as widgets. One thing you should note about the widgets is that they range from pre-processing and data visualization to algorithmic evaluation and predictive modeling.

The Orange widgets play a wide range of roles. These roles include:

- Showing data tables and permitting one to select from a range of features

- Reading of the data

- Training the predictor for a proper comparison of learning algorithms

- Data elements' visualization

The other thing to note about Orange is the fact that it brings a fun vibe and interactive experience to various dull analytic tools within it. The truth is that this tool is quite interesting to operate.

Additionally, the data that comes to Orange is formatted quickly to achieve the desired pattern. They can also be moved easily to where it is required by just flipping or moving the widgets around. When users are using Orange, they are quite fascinated by the experience and the features available. The good thing with this tool is that it offers its users an opportunity to make smart decisions within the shortest time possible as far as data comparison and analysis is concerned.

Weka

This is free software available online. Weka is also referred to as the Waikato Environment named after the University of Waikato, New Zealand where it was first developed. You can use Weka when conducting data analysis as well as predictive modeling. It is composed of algorithms and many visualization tools that offer support to machine learning.

This tool has a Graphical user interface that allows for easy access to all its key features. Just like Rapid Miner, this tool is also written in JAVA programming language. One thing you should note about Weka is that it supports various data mining activities such as data mining, regression, processing and visualization among others.

Weka also works based on the assumption that data is readily available in a flat-file format. It also offers access to SQL databases by way of database connectivity. It can also further process the data returned by a query.

KNIME

This is also an open-source data mining tool that is readily available for use online. This is one of the best integration platforms that you can use for both data reporting and analytics. It was developed by KNIME.com AG. One thing that is important to note about this tool is that it operates based on the concept of a modular data workflow.

KNIME is composed of a wide range of data mining and machine learning components that are embedded within it together. This data mining tool has been extensively used in pharmaceutical research. Additionally, it has a perfect performance when it comes to customer data analysis, business intelligence as well as financial data analysis.

You will note that KNIME has brilliant features that allow for efficient scaling up as well as quick deployment. If you ask many of its users, they will tell you that it takes a short duration to master how to use KNIME and that it offers access to predictive analysis even when you are a naïve user. Finally, KNIME uses an assembly of nodes when doing data pre-processing for both visualization and analytics.

Sisense

Unlike all the other data mining tools we have discussed above, Sisense is an example of a licensed data mining tool. One thing you will note about Sisense is that it is extremely useful and well-suited for BI software as far as reporting goes within the company. Sisense is also named after the company that developed it - "Sisense"

The other thing you will note about Sisense is the fact that is has a brilliant capability of handling and processing data for both small- and large-scale companies. It also permits data combinations from a wide range of sources for the sake of building a common repository. The data is further refined by this tool to generate rich reports that can be shared across a wide range of departments for reporting purposes.

In 2016, Sisense was awarded the best BI software of the year and still holds that good position to date. One thing that makes this tool attractive to users is the fact that it generates reports that are highly visual. Additionally, it is tailor-made for non-technical users with drag & drop features and widgets.

You can also select from a range of widgets to generate reports in the form of bar graphs, pie charts, and line charts depending on the major objective of the organization. You can also drill down the reports further by just clicking on the widgets to check for details as well as comprehensive data.

SQL Server data tools (SSDT)

This tool is also licensed just like the Sisense. It is a universal, declarative model that is known for the expansion of all database development phases in Visual Studio IDE. Formerly, Microsoft developed BIDS for data analysis as well as offer business intelligence solutions. Most developers today use SSDT transact, which is a design capability of SQL, when building, maintaining, debugging and refactoring the databases.

As a user, you can work directly with a database or with a connected database, hence offering an on or off-premise facility. You can also make use of visual studio tools in the development of databases such as code navigation tools, IntelliSense, Visual Basic, and programming support through C#, among others.

Additionally, SSDT offers access to Table Designers that play a significant role when it comes to creating new tables and editing tables directly in the direct database and connected ones. Considering the fact that this tool derives its base from BIDS, which was incompatible with Visual Studio 2010, SSDT BI came to birth and quickly replaced BIDS.

Apache Mahout

This is an open-source data mining tool that is a project developed by Apache Foundation. It plays a primary role in the creation of machine learning algorithms. Its focus is on classification, clustering and collaborative filtering of data.

This tool is written in JAVA programming language and comes with JAVA libraries that are central in performing mathematical operations such as statistics and linear algebra. One thing with this tool is that it is continuously evolving as the algorithms get implemented inside the Apache Mahout.

Unlike the Hadoop, the Mahout algorithms have a higher level of implementation that is achieved by way of mapping or reducing templates. Some of the features this data mining tool possesses include:

- An extensive programming environment
- A math experimentation environment
- Pre-made algorithms
- GPU that play a role in the improvement of performance

Oracle Data Mining

Its availability is a proprietary License. Oracle Data Mining tool is a key component of Oracle Advanced Analytics, which offers excellent data mining algorithms that go a long way in data prediction, classification, specialized analytics and regression among others. This in turn offers its users a deeper analysis insight that makes predictions better, targets the best clients, detects fraud, and identifies cross-selling opportunities that companies can leverage to increase their revenue flow.

One thing you will note about the algorithms developed inside Oracle Data Mining is that they leverage the potential strength that Oracle databases possess. Additionally, the data mining features of SQL have the ability to dig out database tables, views, and schemas among others.

Its graphical user interface (GUI) is simply an extended version of Oracle SQL Developer that offers the drag & drop feature for the data within the database for the user to gain a better insight.

Rattle

This is also an open-source data mining tool that is based on a graphical user interface. It makes use of R stats as its programming language. This explains the reason why it exposes the statistical power of R by offering considerable data mining functionality. Even though Rattle has a well-developed and extensive user interface, it contains an inbuilt log code tab that plays a role in generating duplicate codes for every activity that happens at the graphical user interface.

You can edit and view the dataset that is generated by Rattle. It also offers additional features that allow its users to review the code, use it for a wide range of functions while extending the code beyond restriction.

DataMelt

DataMelt is an open-source data mining tool that is often referred to as DMelt. It plays a significant role as both a computation and visualization environment with an interactive framework for both analysis and visualization of data. In most cases, this tool is tailor-made for scientists, engineers and students.

This tool is written in JAVA programming language and is used on a wide range of platforms. The good thing is that you can also run this data mining tool on any operating system that is compatible with Java Virtual Machine (JVM). It also has scientific and mathematic libraries embedded within it. the scientific libraries are used to draw 2D/3D plots while the mathematical libraries generate random numbers, algorithms, and curve fittings among others. You can also use DMelt when you are analyzing large volumes of data, stat analysis, as well as data mining. In the financial market, engineering and natural science field, this is your go-to tool.

IBM Cognos

This is a proprietary License that is designed as an intelligence suite developed and owned by IBM for the purpose of reporting, score carding, and data analysis. It is also composed of sub-components that are designed to meet the needs and requirements of the organization where it is used. Such sub-components include Cognos connection, report studio, query studio, event studio, analysis studio, and workspace advance.

The Cognos connection is a web portal that is used in gathering and summarizing data in reports as well as scoreboards. Query studio contains queries that are important in creating diagrams and formatting data. The report studio, on the other hand, generates management reports.

The Analysis Studio is important in processing large data volumes, understanding them and then identifying trends/patterns. The Event Studio plays a role in notifying modules to keep in sync with a wide range of events. Workspace Advanced is also a user-friendly interface component that is used when creating personalized and user-friendly documents.

IBM SPSS Modeler

This is a proprietary license tool that is owned by IBM. This tool plays a role in data mining and text analytics for the purpose of establishing a predictive model. This was originally developed by SPSS Inc. but was later acquired by IBM, hence a combination of names from both companies.

One thing you will note about SPSS Modeler is the fact that it has a visual interface that permits its users to work with data mining algorithms without necessarily requiring programming. It also tries to eliminate all unnecessary complexities that one faces during data transformation making it easy for use in predictive models.

This modeler comes in two editions, namely IBM SPSS Modeler professional and IBM SPSS Modeler Premium that contains a wide range of additional features like entity analytics and text analytics.

SAS Data Mining

This is also a proprietary license data mining tool that is produced by the SAS Institute. This tool was mainly developed for data management and analytics. One thing with this tool is that it can mine data, change it, manage it for varied sources and performing statistical analysis. It also offers a graphical user interface that is friendly with non-technical users.

The SAS data miner provides users with big data analysis tools, allowing for accurate insights that help in making timely decisions. SAS comprises a scalable, distributed architecture for processing memory, making this tool the best choice as far as text mining, data mining and optimizations are concerned.

Teradata

This is licensed and is often referred to as the Teradata database. It is an enterprise data warehouse that contains a wide range of data management tools with data mining software you can use for business analytics.

One thing that is important to note about Teradata is that it offers a deeper insight into a company's sales data, product placement as well as customer-preference among others. It also plays a significant role in differentiating hot from cold data, which simply means that it places data that is less frequently used in a slow storage section of the database.

Finally, the Teradata mining tool operates on "share nothing" architecture considering the fact that it has a server node with their memory and processing capability.

Board

Its availability is Proprietary License. It is often referred to as the Board toolkit. Board is a software that is developed for business intelligence analytics as well as corporate performance management. One thing you will note is that most companies looking to boost their decision making employ the use of this tool. This is mainly because the Board is known to gather up data from a wide range of sources, streamlines the data, and generates reports in formats that are preferred by the company.

It also is characterized by an attractive and comprehensible interface among all BI software available in the industry. This is what allows it to offer facilities that perform multi-dimensional analysis, track performance planning as well as control workflows.

Dundas BI

This is also a licensed data mining tool that has an excellent dashboard, data analytics and reporting tools. It is known for its reliability with quick integration and insights. It offers unlimited transformation patterns of data with attractive tables, graphs and charts. They also offer fantastic features that allow for accessibility of data from all sources with documents that have gap-free protection.

Additionally, this data mining tool has well-defined structures that are specifically ordered for ease of processing. They also have relational methods that allow for multi-dimensional analysis that focuses mainly on business-critical matters. As reliable reports are generated, the cost is reduced, and the requirements of other additional software are eliminated.

Chapter 12

Text Mining in Data Mining: Process and Applications

This technique is also referred to as text data mining. The main point of text mining is to process unstructured information, with the aim of to extract numerical indices that have some meaning from texts. The end result here is to ensure that the information from the text can be accessed easily by various data mining algorithms.

One thing you need to note is that the information you extract can be used in deriving summaries of the words contained in the documents, with consideration given to words contained in them. This means that you can analyze words as well as the cluster of words that have been used in the documents. Additionally, you can choose to analyze the documents to elucidate the similarities between them as well as the manner in which they are related to other variables of interest in the data mining project in question.

Generally, think of text mining as the conversion of texts into numbers. These numbers are then incorporated in other analyses as well as the application of unsupervised learning methods like clustering.

Some of the areas where text mining is used include:

Information Extraction

This simply refers to an extension to the retrieval of documents, i.e. the returned documents are condensed, followed by a summary of the text that focuses on the user's query.

Information retrieval plays a significant role in narrowing the documents down to those that are important in resolving a specific problem. One thing you need to bear in mind is that text mining concerns itself with the application of complex algorithms to a large collection of documents. Additionally, information retrieval speeds up the process of data analysis by lowering the document number significantly.

Data Mining

Well, this is a book about data mining. However, one thing that you have to understand is that you cannot discuss data mining without touching on text mining, and vice versa. The point here is to identify patterns in the data. This step will focus mainly on categorizing and characterizing the extraction process of hidden data. With the use of data mining tools, you can accurately predict the behaviors as well as future trends.

It also plays a significant role in businesses as far as positive and knowledge-based decisions are concerned. The truth is that data mining tools will help you answer critical business questions that have typically been time-consuming in the past. This is by searching the databases to seek out any hidden patterns that are unknown.

Natural Language Processing (NLP)

One thing you will realize is that NLP is an age-old, extremely challenging problem. It is nothing more than a study of human language and it means that we can train computers in a way they are able to comprehend natural language in the same way that humans do.

NLP tends to be used as a way of understanding how humans understand particular documents or sentences - think about how we understand what someone did and to whom. The main aim of NLP, as far as text mining goes, is to ensure that the system is delivered, in the data extraction phase, as an input.

Information Extraction

This simply refers to a task that involves the automatic extraction of structured data/information for unstructured ones. In many cases, this involves the processing of the human language texts by way of NLP.

Text mining process

The process of text data mining often includes activities that help in information or data mining, including:

Step 1: Text-Processing

The first thing that you do here is text cleanup, which is all about removing any unwanted and unnecessary information present in the dataset. Some of this information includes things like ads from web pages, normalize texts that are converted from the binary format.

The next thing is to perform tokenization. To do this, the texts are split into white spaces. Finally, you do speech tagging, using POS, or parts-of-speech, as token assignments. The input in this case is provided by the tokenized text. Therefore, the taggers are required to manage unknown words and ambiguous mappings for word tags.

Step 2: Text Transformation

This is also referred to as attribute generation. In this case, words contained in a text document are used to represent that document as well as their specific occurrences. Here, you can use two major approaches for documenting the representations. These approaches include a bag-of-words and vector space.

Step 3: Feature Selection

This is also referred to as attribute or variable selection. It refers to the selection of a specific subset containing important features that you can use in creating the model. In this case, any features that do not provide additional information are called "redundant". On the other hand, the irrelevant features will not give you any useful or relevant information irrespective of what context you are looking at.

Step 4:Data Mining

At this particular point, the process of text mining merges with the standard processes. Here, standard techniques for data mining are applied in handling structured databases.

Step 5: Evaluation

Once you get the results you are looking for, the next thing is for you to evaluate the outcome and then discard the results once your evaluation is complete.

Approaches to Text Mining in Data Mining

In order to understand text mining results, you have to use a method that is been tried and tested. Once the data matrix is ready. Computed using the input document, you can apply a wide range of analytical techniques to process the data. This is inclusive of methods that are used in data clustering.

Just to reiterate, you can say that text mining is the process of summarizing texts in the numeric format. At its core, all the words that are found in the input document are counted and indexed so that a table of the words and documents are computed. In other words, a matrix that shows how often each word occurs in the document.

One thing you need to bear in mind is that you can further refine the process to ensure that it excludes certain words that are common like "a" and "the". Then they can combine the grammatical forms of each word, like "traveled" and "travel", among others. Once you get a table containing the unique words, you can then proceed to apply all the standard data mining and statistical techniques, allowing you to derive clusters and dimensions of words or documents, or a set of important words that may be used for predicting the outcome variable you want.

Using tried and tested methods is the best step towards understanding the outcome of text mining. One thing you need to understand is that once the input document has been used to compute the data matrix, you can use a wide range of analytical tools to process the data further. Some of these include predictive data mining, clustering and factoring among others.

The other approach here is the black-box approach to text mining and concept extraction. Several text mining applications offer black-box methods for extraction of the deeper meaning from the documents with little to no effort at all. The thing with these applications is that they rely solely on proprietary algorithms in the extraction of concepts from texts. They may even claim the ability to summarize large numbers of text documents automatically. This way, the core and the most important parts of the document are retained.

While there are so many algorithmic approaches to the extraction of meaning from a document, the truth is that this type of technology is still at its infancy. Additionally, the inspiration to provide meaningful summaries of large numbers of the document may very much still be elusive. In that case, we often urge skepticism when using such kind of algorithms. The reasons for this include:

- Result interpretation is not really possible if the users are not clear on how the algorithms work

- The methods utilized in the program cannot be scrutinized. For instance, the peer review or academic community and hence, we may not know how well they are likely to perform in various field

Now, just to summarize this section, the most important thing you need to do is try out the various automated translation services that are available on the web. This is to find those that are capable of translating the whole paragraph of your text from one language to another.

From there, attempt to translate some texts especially the simple ones into your native language and then back. Now, look at the results. What you will notice is that almost every time they try translating the shorter sentences into another language, and then back to the original, retaining the first language, the results are rarely accurate; rather, they can be quite humorous. This simply illustrates the challenge in interpreting the meaning of a text.

Finally, text mining as a document search is another approach you can use. Using this approach, you are automatically searching a large number of documents on the basis of the key phrases and words used. This is what the internet uses today; the algorithm has been developed over time to ensure the search engine offers efficient and fast access to the web pages by narrowing down the content to specifically what you are interested in finding.

How Do You Numericize Texts?

There are so many ways in which you can numericize texts and we have already seen the various steps you can employ. However, the most important thing you will notice is that there are so many considerations that you have to factor in when you are numericizing texts. These include:

A large number of large documents

We have already seen scenarios where we used many small documents. Here, if you are considering concept extraction from a small number of larger documents, you will note that the analysis is not so powerful because there are fewer use cases. On the other hand, the number of variables (in this case extracted words) is very large.

Excluding Certain Numbers, Short Words and Characters

One thing you will note is that the exclusion of specific characters and numbers can be easily done. However, this must be done before the input documents are indexed. It may also be important if you excluded rare words that only occur in a small portion of the document after processing.

Include Lists, Exclude Lists

These are also referred to as stop-words. This is especially very useful if you are searching for a specific word or if you are classifying the input document on the basis of frequency. The stops are simply the words that you use when excluding from the indexing. Some of the default stop words in English include "the", "a", "of", and "since", among others, which are frequently used but then carry very little information about what the document contains.

Synonyms and Phrases

These are words like "sick", or "ill" that only get used in specific phrases to mean the same things. Here, they can be used to denote unique meanings but then are combined for the sake of indexing.

For instance, one such phrase can be Microsoft Windows. When you hear of this term, the first thing that comes to mind is the windows operating system. However, it has nothing to do with the term, "windows", that is commonly used when we talk about home improvements.

Support for Different Languages

Synonyms, Stemming, etc., are simply letters that are allowed in words. The thing about these words is that they are considered to be operations that are highly dependent on language. That said, support for a wide range of languages is very important.

Stemming Algorithm

This is a very critical pre-processing step that is performed prior to indexing the input document. The term stemming often refers to reducing a word down to its root, mostly seen when converting the different words into grammatical formats.

Incorporating Text Mining Results

This is usually done once you have extracted significant words from the input documents or when decomposition of a singular value is applied to the extraction of semantic dimensions. After this, you can begin using the information you extracted.

In this case you can use:

Graphics

Also referred to as visual methods. This often depends on why the analysis is being done. In such a case, extracting the semantic dimensions is the only requirement. This is mainly because it is considered a very useful tool in clarifying the underlying structure of your dataset.

Clustering and Factoring

The main role of this step is to ensure that you can identify sets of documents as well as similar sets of the input text. This form of analysis is often conducted in market research, such as determining new home buyers. In this case, you could use techniques like classification analysis, factor analysis, as well as principal components.

Predictive Data Mining

This allows you to use the raw data as the predictor variables when you work on a data mining project.

Text Mining Applications

It is very common to come across unstructured text and this might represent a majority of information available from a wide range of research studies. Text mining can be used in various areas like:

Analysis of Open-Ended Survey Responses

When you are conducting survey research, it is very common to include a number of flexible questions that relate to the specific topic, allowing those surveyed to give their unrestricted views, without constraint.

Automatic message and email processing

Here, text mining can be used when automatically classifying texts in emails or messages. For instance, you can choose to filter out the junk emails. To do this, you can choose specific words or terms not likely to appear in any message that is legitimate.

Rather than identifying electronic mails that are undesirable, you can automatically choose to discard these messages. It is through automated classification systems for electronic messages that can be used with text mining. This way, you can route the right message to the right department. You can also screen for any inappropriate messages so that they are sent back with the request to eliminate the offending content or words.

Analyzing Warrant, Insurance Claims and Diagnostic Interviews

If you look at most business domains, you will be surprised to find that a majority of the information here is collected in an open-ended format.

For instance, when dealing with claims or medical interviews, they are often summarized very briefly. What is interesting is the fact that these notes are electronically gathered so that they are immediately ready to be input. As far as the medical field goes, flexible descriptions can be given on patient symptoms that are then used as clues of what the actual diagnosis may be.

Crawling the Website Investigating Competitors

The other application of text mining is the processing of content derived from web pages in a certain domain. For instance, you can go to a web page and then start looking through the links to process all the web pages referenced. This way, you come up with a list of all the relevant results that are available on the site.

Advantages of Text Mining

Text mining has so many advantages that are associated with it, which explains the reason why it is gaining so much popularity among corporations and government agencies. It is through text mining that e-commerce has had the capability to do personalized marketing. This is mainly because it consists of results derived from higher trade volumes.

Additionally, government agencies are currently using these kinds of technologies when classifying threats. It is this kind of predicting capability that goes a long way in benefiting society through quick identification of criminal activities. The companies are also able to establish better customer relationships by offering them exactly what they need as the companies can better understand what their clients want and react to those needs faster and effectively.

Disadvantages of Text Mining

One thing that you need to understand is that text mining in itself does not create lots of issues. However, when this is applied to data of a personalized nature, there may be concerns that arise. The most criticized ethical issue of all time is associated with privacy.

The privacy of an individual is often considered lost if the information concerning that individual is obtained, analyzed and then clustered into profiles. Additionally, the data is known to create anonymous clustering to ensure that no individual links directly to the profile.

However, the issue is that these group profiles are often treated as a personal profile, something that ends up de-individualizing the user. This way, they are just judged by their mouse clicks.

But what is de-individualization?

Well, this can be defined as the tendency of treating people by judging them as you see fit most especially based on group characteristics.

The other important concern is that associated with companies that are collecting the data for a particular purpose and then turn back and uses that data for a totally different purpose altogether. What this does is that it violates the interests of the users.

With the growing trend of selling personal data as a commodity, this encourages a lot of identity theft and the chances of one's privacy being invaded.

Chapter 13

Data Modeling in Data Mining?

W hen you think of data mining, you can't help but think about data modeling, right? Yeah well, most people don't think about this until the time when they have to model the data before storing them in the database. So, the million-dollar question here is, what is data modeling?

Data modeling simply refers to the process of building data models for the data prior to storing them in the database. In other words, think of data modeling as a conceptual representation of such things as data objects, rules and associations between a wide range of data objects.

One thing you need to bear in mind is that data modeling plays a critical role in visualizing the data and enforcement of governmental and business policies and compliance with regulations. In other words, data models ensure that there is consistency in the manner in which data is named, default values, security and semantics while still upholding the quality requirements of the data.

The role of data models is to emphasize what the data requires and the manner in which it should be ordered rather than what operations are to be performed on the data. It helps to think of data models as architects constructing a building such that the conceptual model is created to set the relationship between the various data items.

The two most common types of data models' techniques are:

- Unified modeling language (UML)

- Entity-relationship models (E-RM)

Why Use Data Models?

This makes us think about the major goals of setting up data models in the first place. Well, one of the most important things that come to mind when you think of data models is the fact that they ensure all the data that are needed by the database are represented accurately. This is because if the data is omitted, there will be the creation of faulty reports which will ultimately yield incorrect results.

The other thing is, a data model plays an important role in designing the database at its conceptual, logical and physical level. They also define the relational tables, foreign and primary keys as well as any stored procedures in the database.

Data models also pain a clear picture of the base data that can be used by developers of the database when creating a physical database. It also is helpful in the identification of missing and redundant data. Note that despite the fact that the initial creation of the data models is labor-intensive and time-consuming, it plays a role in upgrading the IT infrastructure and in ensuring faster and cheaper maintenance.

Types of Data models

There are three major data model types. These are:

Conceptual Data Models

This data model simply defines what is in the system. Typically, it is created by both data architects and business stakeholders. The main purpose of this is the organization, definition and provision of the scope of the business concepts and rules.

One of the major aims of this kind of model is the establishment of the entities, attributes and relationships between data items. At this level of data modeling, there is very little available detail about the actual structure of the database.

The three tenants of this model are entity, attributes, and relationships. Entity refers to real-world objects. Attributes are entity properties and features, while relationships refer to associations or dependencies between two or more entities.

For instance, customers and products are two entities, while the customer umbers and names are entities. Product price and name are product attributes and a sale is a client-product relationship.

Features of the conceptual data model

- One thing about this type of data model is that it offers organization-wide coverage when it comes to business concepts

- They are developed specifically for the business audience

- Hardware specifications are not taken into account during development - location, storage capacity, and software specifications (e.g. DBMS technology and vendor). The main aim here is to represent data as a user would perceive it in the real world.

Logical Data Models

The main aim of the logical data models is to define how the system is supposed to be implemented irrespective of the database management system (DBMS). This model is typically created by both business analysts and data architects. The main aim is to come up with technical maps of data structures and rules.

One thing that is important to bear in mind is that logical data models add deeper insight into the conceptual data model elements. This is by defining the structure of the data elements and then setting the relationship between them.

One of the advantages of using logical data models is to offer a solid foundation that forms the basis for the physical model while retaining a generic structure.

At the level of data modeling, there is no definition of the primary and secondary keys. At this level, what is required is a verification and adjustment of connector details set earlier for the relationship.

Features of a logical data model

- It describes the needs of the data for one project but other data models may be integrated, depending on the project scope.

- They are designed and independently developed from the database management system (DBMS).

- Data attributes in this case have data-types with exact length and precision

- The normalization process of the model is typically applied to the third normal factor (3NF)

Physical Data Models

This is important in helping us know how the system will be implemented using a specific database management system (DBMS). This model is typically created by DBA as well as developers. The main purpose here is the actual implementation of the database.

One thing that is important to note about a physical data model is that it describes a specific implementation of the model. It also plays an important role in the abstraction of the database which helps in generating the schema and rich metadata.

Data models like this also go a long way in helping in the visualization of database structures. This is by modeling the database column keys, indexes, triggers, constraints and other features.

Features of a physical data model

- It gives a description of the data needs of a single application or project despite the fact that you can integrate it with other data models, depending on the scope of the project.

- This data model specifies table relationships that address relationship nullability and cardinality

- It is often built for a specific version of a database management system, data storage, location, and technology applied to the project.

- The primary and the foreign keys, indices, views, authorizations, and access profiles are defined by the physical data model

- Columns in this case have exact lengths assigned, data types, as well as default values.

Data Modeling Approaches

To this point, we can comfortably see that data modeling is a painstakingly upfront process. This explains why it sometimes appears to be divided from methods used in rapid development. Today, agile programming is used extensively for speeding up project development where data modeling is adopted.

Think of data models as being flowcharts showing the relationship between different data types. It helps the stakeholders pinpoint mistakes/errors while ensuring that changes are made prior to writing program code and running it. Alternatively, where reverse engineering is used, data models may be used to extract models from systems that are already in use, such as NoSQL data.

The role of the data modelers is to use a wide range of data models in viewing similar data to make sure that the processes, relationships, entities and data flows are identified accurately. New projects are initiated by collecting all requirements from the business stakeholders. In other words, you can break down data modeling stages by creating logical data models that demonstrate specific attributes, relationships and entities, and physical data models.

It is important to note that logical data models play a role as the foundation on which physical data models are created. This is application-specific as well as being specific to the database under implementation.

Approach 1: Hierarchical Modeling

The hierarchical data model arrays data in the form of a tree. It is a one-to-many arrangement that came in to replace the file-based system in many use cases. IBM's Information Management System is a very good example showing the hierarchical approach to data modeling. This is mostly applied in businesses like the banking sector.

Despite the fact that hierarchical data models are greatly superseded by relational models this approach is still very common in the Extensible Markup Language (XML) and Geographical Information Systems (GIS).

It is important to bear in mind that the network models were designed when Database Management Systems were first developed a way of providing a broad, conceptual system view to data designers. A good example of this is the Conference on Data Systems Languages (CODASYL), aimed at bringing about the standardization of programming languages used across several computer systems.

Approach 2: Relational Modeling

One thing to note about this approach is that it played a central role in reducing program complexity as opposed to the file-based system. This modeling approach was brought in as an alternative method to hierarchical data modeling. However, in this case developers are not required to define the data paths.

What you will note about the relational modeling was that it was used where tables are used to join data segments. This is quite the opposite of the hierarchical model, in which the data is joined implicitly. After inception, relational data models were coupled with structured query language (SQL), which contributed to it gaining more of a foothold for Enterprise computing, to facilitate efficient data processing.

Approach 3: The Entity-Relationship Model

This approach is known to have taken a bigger step in the 1970s as the use of the entity-relationship model which led to its popularity in the business world. The entity and relational data models are amalgamated in that the entity models make use of diagrams that graphically demonstrate the database elements while making it easy to understand the underlying models.

In relational data models, the data types are defined and do not change over time. Note that entities are composed of attributes, such as employee entity's attributes, that include such things as a name – both first and last, and time of employment, among others. It is critical to note that relationships are often mapped visually so that the design objectives can easily communicate with various participants in both data maintenance and development.

This model also gained object-oriented programming features that helped in designing systems. While it bears the resemblance to ERs methods, object-oriented kind of approach often differs in the sense that they pay attention to object abstraction in real-world entities.

In this case, objects are often grouped into class hierarchies, with the objects inside them inheriting the methods and the attributes of their parent classes. As such, this approach ensures that data integrity is upheld, and the complex relationships retain support.

Approach 4: Graph Models

This is a branch that, with a combination of graph databases and the network and/or hierarchical data models, provides a description of the more complex dataset relationships. This is especially the case with the fraud detection and the social media applications, as well as recommenders among others.

The graph model provides a graph, connecting the nodes and the relationships in the same way as they would an ER model. This kind of model is often used in text analysis, building new models that reveal hidden relationships between the data points in a document.

Advantages of Data Models

- They make certain that the data objects offered by the functional team are accurately represented

- They are quite detailed for use in constructing physical databases

- The information contained in the data models are very useful in defining the relationship between foreign and primary keys, tables as well as stored procedures

- They help a great deal in streamlining communication within and across various organizations

- They document the data mappings in the ETL process

- They help in recognizing the correct data sources that would be useful in populating the model

Disadvantages of Data Models
- To develop the data models, it is critical that one knows the features of the physical data stored

- It is thought of as a navigational system that often produces complex applications management and development that requires one to know the biographical truth

- Even a smaller change made in the data structure needs a modification in the whole application

- There is no set data manipulation language in the database management system (DBMS)

Chapter 14

Data Mining and the Current Market

Data Mining Market Size

According to Giga's research, the data mining market has already hit the billion-dollar mark. This is inclusive of services and software used in data mining. In business intelligence alone, data mining represents about 15% of the market. What is interesting to note is that data mining is quickly evolving from transitional packages to data mining applications, ERP, integrated CRM and other business applications.

There are many different data mining products on the market. In the previous chapter, we have discussed some of the data mining tools that you can use. Some of those tools are produced by the companies we will discuss in this section to highlight the size of the market represented by data mining. KDNuggets has a long list of all the companies that offer data mining products. Some of these companies include:

SAS

This is probably one of the largest data mining vendors based on the number of market shares it owns. For several decades, SAS has been in the field of statistics. One thing you should note about the SAS base is that it is provides a wide range of statistical functions you can employ when performing a wide range of data analysis tasks.

Additionally, the SAS Scripting language is one of the most powerful. Its enterprise miner was born in 1997 and has since grown into a multi-million dollar enterprise. It offers a range of data mining algorithms like regression, association, decision trees, and neural networks among others. It also offers support for text mining tasks.

SPSS

Another of the large statistics organizations, SPSS offers a wide range of data mining products like Answer trees and SPSS base. In 1998, the organization acquired ISL (a UK-based company) along with its Clementine data mining package.

At the time, Clementine was an industry leader in introducing the data mining workflows that helped its users clean and transform data, as well as train models using the very workflow environment. The good thing about Clementine was the fact that it offered a wide range of tools important in managing data mining project cycles.

IBM

IBM has a wide range of data mining tools, some of which we have discussed in the previous chapter. With IBM there is a data mining product referred to as Intelligent miner. This data mining tool is composed of visualization tools and algorithms. What this tool does is to export mining models in a predictive modeling markup language (PMML), originally characterized by the data mining group (DMG).

The PMML documents are simply extensible markup language files that contain model pattern descriptions and statistics that can be used to train the dataset. The good thing is, the DB2 database can load these files.

Microsoft Corporation

Of all those present in the market, the first leading vendor to add data mining into their relational database was Microsoft. For instance, SQL server 2000 contains at least two data mining algorithms that are patented. These algorithms are the Microsoft decision tree and Microsoft clustering.

Aside from the algorithms, the next most important data mining feature was the OLE DB, which refers to the industry-standard whose major role is to define a data mining language in the same style as SQL, as well as a set of schema's rowsets targeting database developers.

It is through this API that data mining components can be embedded, like prediction features into the user applications.

Oracle

Oracle 9i was released in 2000 and contains several algorithms for data mining based on the Naïve Bayes and Association techniques. On the other hand, Oracle 10g has a wide range of tools and algorithms for data mining purposes. The other thing about oracle is that it incorporates JAVA data mining API, which is a JAVA package designed to perform various data mining tasks.

Angoss

One of the data mining tools produced by this company includes the knowledge studio which is well known for performing data mining activities including constructing a decision tree, cluster analysis as well as predictive models. It also plays a significant role in helping users mine data from a wide range of perspectives and to understand it.

Angoss also has powerful data visualization tools that support and explain their discoveries. They also have content viewer controls that work well with data mining algorithms in SQL server 2000. The good thing is that you can plug its algorithms into the SQL server platform.

KXEN

This is a French company providing data mining software. It offers access to a wide range of data mining algorithms such as regression, segmentation, SVM and time series among others. They also offer OLAP cube data mining solutions and it is also known for developing an Excel plug-in that gives users a friendly environment for their data mining projects.

Chapter 15

New Trends in Data Mining?

If you compare data mining to database technology, you will be surprised to learn that data mining is much younger. In fact, it is thought of as an emerging market and niche. One reason for this is the fact that most packages are aimed at data miners and statisticians. However, most application developers often consider these technologies too hard to truly master.

Recently, several data mining vendors like Microsoft, grasped this fact and developed a number of APIs specific to data mining. That is why it is projected that in the coming years, the number of developers will have increased tremendously to build data mining models. What this means is that there will be many applications available in the market, most of which will have features relating to data mining. .

What is important to note is that most of the businesses that have been slow in adopting data mining processes are beginning to catch up with the others. What businesses are doing today is extracting critical information through data mining processes to inform their business decision-making.

This is why in the coming years, we can expect data mining to become ubiquitous as one of the most prevalent technologies in the market. Here are some of the key data mining trends anticipated in the future:

Embedded Data Mining

Going forward, many Enterprise applications are expected to include a wide range of data mining features. Most of these features are likely to be prediction features that add value to the tools.

For instance, CRM applications are expected to allow many users to predict their product sales. This way, online retailers can have the ability to recommend their products to target clients for the sake of cross-selling. This is very much the case where industrial or Enterprise-scale data mining APIs, such as OLE DB, allows database developers to use and embed their data mining features in business applications.

The biggest advantage of this is that it will bring about the growth of the data mining market. Who says no to that!

Data Mining Packages for Vertical Applications

The addition of the database management system (DBMS) packages by major database vendors around the globe is expected to become increasingly popular in the coming years. The main reason is that data mining has the potential of being applied in almost all sectors. Today, data mining is in the telecom, finance and insurance industries.

That said, there is an ever-expanding requirement for specialized techniques, designed to help people and businesses address problems they currently face in a wide range of vertical industries. For instance, the healthcare industry needs special data mining techniques that will help them in the analysis of DNA sequences. On the other hand, network security applications require algorithms trained in real time, used in the detection of network intrusion and breach.

In other words, the world that we live in is one that churns out so much information and data by the minute. This means that non-traditional data mining techniques are needed to aid in the analysis of unstructured data posted into the Worldwide Web.

The other vertical sector is text mining, which requires specialized data mining tools and algorithms. The traditional horizontal data mining tools that we already have are not advanced enough to handle such kind of problems. This will lead to new packages specializing in vertical sectors and their problems.

Product Consolidation

Looking at many of the software vendors of today, we can see that most of their software is packages related to data mining but they only have a couple of algorithms in them. There is still a great deal of fragmentation in the market and just like any other software sector, consolidation is inevitable. This is mainly because small software vendors will face stiff competition from fellow small software vendors. This is especially the case when major database vendors add the data mining features to their database management systems (DBMS).

PMML

Despite the fact that big vendors like Oracle, SAS, Microsoft, and IBM among others compete on a wide range of data mining APIs, the truth is that they are all members of the Data Mining Group (DMG).

In other words, when you keenly look at each of these companies in the market, they offer support to the PMML as their model persistence format. This is mainly because PMML offers various advantages as far as model exchange and deployment goes. Considering that it is an XML document, it allows advanced users to edit. Very soon, it is expected that PMML will be trending big.

Multimedia Data Mining

Today, multimedia data mining is catching on considering the growing ability to accurately capture useful data. This involves extracting data from a wide range of multimedia sources such as texts, images, hypertexts, videos among others. This data is then converted into a numerical format. This way, they can now be used in classification and clustering, the performance of similarity checks, as well as identification of associations.

Ubiquitous Data Mining

This simply refers to a method used in mining data from mobile devices to gather information about the user. In spite of the fact that there are so many challenges in this, this method offers quite an opportunity to go big in various industries such as studies of human-computer interactions. Some of these challenges include complexity, cost, and privacy among others.

Distributed Data Mining

This is one of the trends that is quickly gaining popularity in the market. This is mainly because it involves mining of huge amounts of information stored in varied locations in the company or those that are stored in different organizations. Highly sophisticated algorithms are currently being used in data extraction from varied locations. The good news is that this data offers insight and reports based on them.

Spatial and Geographical Data Mining

This is also a new trending type of data mining that involves the extraction of information from the surrounding astronomical and geographical data that also includes images collected from outer space. It is this kind of data mining that plays a critical role in revealing various aspects of the environment like topology and distance, which is mainly used in geographical information systems (GIS) and, among others, navigation applications.

Trends in Data Mining Techniques

As we have already seen in this chapter, data mining evolves very quickly, with new, better techniques emerging regularly to fine-tune the current concepts. This evolution is important because it allows companies to have continually evolving insight into their own data, providing future trends that will be useful.

Some of the techniques employed by the data experts include the following:

Seeking Out Incomplete Data

One thing that is important to note is that data mining is reliant on the data – if it isn't there, or it isn't complete, the results will not be true. Therefore, it is essential to have an intelligence system that will sniff out incomplete data as much as possible.

Some of the techniques, like Self-Organizing-Maps (SOM's), play a major role in mapping out missing data through visualization where the data is multi-dimensional. Multi-task machine learning comprises a valid, complete dataset being compared to an incomplete one in an attempt to locate the missing values.

The thing is that these multi-dimensional preceptors use intelligent algorithms in building an imputation technique whose main role is to address the incomplete attributes of the dataset.

Dynamic Data Dashboards

This is simply a scoreboard that is present on a manager's computer. The scoreboard is given the data as it arrives from the company databases, with data mining techniques providing real-time insights to the company stakeholders.

Database Analysis

Most databases contain structured data so the algorithms that look for the hidden patterns are usually built into the data flows; this ensures that the information they glean is immediately placed into a report in a meaningful data analysis.

Text Analysis

This is one of the most important concepts in finding patterns automatically within texts that are embedded in other files, such as text. ,doc, PDF, and presentation, like PowerPoint. Algorithms designed to process text can look for repeated data which can help educational facilities to find plagiarized content.

Efficient Handling of Complex and Relational Data

It is important that data warehouses or large databases are supported with both interactive and query-based data mining techniques that will help in such data mining functions as clustering, classification, prediction, and association.

One of the most useful methodologies currently in use is the OLAP (Online Analytical Processing). Other concepts that help in interactive data mining include the use of aggregate queries, graphs, swap randomization, image classification, multi-dimensional statistical analysis, and meta-rule guided mining among others.

Relevance and Scalability of Selected Data Mining Algorithms

When choosing the best data mining algorithm to use, one of the most important things for enterprises to bear in mind is the relevance of the business predictions as well as scalability for the sake of minimizing costs.

This simply means that multiple algorithms are to be used in parallel for time efficiency and independently to avoid interfering with transnational business applications. In other words, there should be support for features like SVM on large databases.

Conclusion

After all is said, one thing that we need to remember is that data is all around us and it is this very data that drives the world. Look around the businesses established within our surroundings and one thing you will not miss for sure is their dependence on data of some sort. Most businesses consider revenue and expense data when making informed business decisions that will help them keep the business profitable.

One thing you will notice is that businesses are focusing their attention on the sales numbers and using these numbers to predict peak times as well as in optimizing stock levels. Are you wondering why they want to learn more and more about their data? At this point, you already know the importance of data mining for companies and organizations alike. You have seen how various data mining techniques go a long way in helping push the businesses forward.

On the other hand, the use of a data mining enrolment management system is something that is beginning to gain popularity in the data mining field. What you will notice is that current data mining is primarily categorical and numerical data. However, this is not going to remain the same for too long. The future trends are beginning to show with data mining including more complex data types.

For any models that have been designed, the best thing is for refinement which is possible through an examination of a wide range of variables and their relationships. According to research, it is evident that data mining will probably result in new methods that will help in the determination of interesting features of the data. With the development of data models and their subsequent implementation, they can be actively used in the enrolment management.

Indeed, data mining is very useful in the world of today in so many ways possible. You can apply it when marketing and when you are aiming at determining the behaviors of customers. This way, you can start mining data by advertising and getting closer to your target clients. This way, you will not only identify trends of customers for the readily available good in the market, but also allow you as a retailer to understand the purchasing power and behavior of your target audience.

In the education domain, you can use data mining in determining the learning behaviors of your students as well as that of the learning institutions in relation to those that are competing with them. This way, institutions can start using the available data in upgrading their modules and courses accordingly.

We can also use data mining in resolving natural disasters. Say we collect information from previous disasters, we can then use what we already have in the database to predict likely events to happen in the future. This way, we can start putting measures in place to ensure that these natural disasters do not affect people living within the areas.

From what we have already gathered in this book, it is clear that we can use data mining in delivering tremendous business insights with regard to challenges that business is facing as well as identifying and leveraging new opportunities. However, one thing that we need to bear in mind is that more research is required to measure the benefits of data mining. If there is a chance that managers are not able to quality these benefits, then they have to take a step further to justify the high cost. With a better justification, more and more legitimate tools will be developed.

The truth is that with data management, the same process needs to be applied across organizations using carious organizational development tools. Once data mining processes have been implemented, it is the responsibility of the company to take the required steps in monitoring the process, obtaining feedback and developing corrective strategies that will help the company out of potential pitfalls.

So, what are you planning to do with your company's data? Take advantage of the data mining techniques we have discussed and start influencing change and growth today.

Best of Luck!

* 9 7 8 1 7 1 3 2 0 5 3 3 3 *